ROUTLEDGE LIBRARY EDITIONS:
MONETARY ECONOMICS

Volume 8

MONETARY POLICY AND CRISES

MONETARY POLICY AND CRISES

A Study of Swedish Experience

BRINLEY THOMAS

Routledge
Taylor & Francis Group
LONDON AND NEW YORK

First published in 1936 by George Routledge and Sons, Ltd.

This edition first published in 2017
by Routledge
2 Park Square, Milton Park, Abingdon, Oxon OX14 4RN

and by Routledge
605 Third Avenue, New York, NY 10017

Routledge is an imprint of the Taylor & Francis Group, an informa business

British Library Cataloguing in Publication Data
A catalogue record for this book is available from the British Library

ISBN: 978-1-138-73264-3 (Set)
ISBN: 978-1-315-16457-1 (Set) (ebk)
ISBN: 978-1-138-63432-9 (Volume 8) (hbk)

Publisher's Note
The publisher has gone to great lengths to ensure the quality of this reprint but points out that some imperfections in the original copies may be apparent.

Disclaimer
The publisher has made every effort to trace copyright holders and would welcome correspondence from those they have been unable to trace.

MONETARY POLICY AND CRISES

A STUDY OF SWEDISH EXPERIENCE

BY

BRINLEY THOMAS

M.A., Ph.D.

LONDON

GEORGE ROUTLEDGE AND SONS, LTD.

BROADWAY HOUSE, CARTER LANE, E.C.

1936

PRINTED IN GREAT BRITAIN BY
STEPHEN AUSTIN AND SONS, LIMITED, HERTFORD

To

My Father and Mother

CONTENTS

PREFACE

THE making of this book began when the author was awarded an Acland Travelling Scholarship, tenable in Sweden from October, 1933, to April, 1934.[1] He went to study Swedish economic thought and experience, particularly as regards money and public finance. He has gone back more than once, most recently in September, 1935, and, having learned Swedish, has kept his knowledge of events up to date. The result is a book of quite exceptional interest.

Judged by any sensible standard, Sweden is one of the most civilized countries in the world. And in the field of economics, as in many other fields, both Swedish theory and Swedish practice are highly distinguished. Economists in that country are, and have long been, in closer touch with practical affairs than in some others, with benefit both to themselves and to public policy. They seem, moreover, as a class, to have a better public reputation than elsewhere. And individually, to-day not less than yesterday, they make their mark on

[1] This book is, in some degree, a sequel to *Unbalanced Budgets: a Study of the Financial Crisis in Fifteen Countries* (Routledge, 1934), to which Dr. Brinley Thomas contributed a valuable section on Germany. See also my Preface to that book for an account of the origin and character of the Acland Trust.

the intellectual life, not only of their own small country, but of the world. Yesterday Wicksell, Cassel, and Davidson ; to-day Myrdal, Lindahl, and Ohlin.

This book is, in part, an instructive chapter in economic history ; in part, a stimulating chapter in the history of economic thought. But, best of all, it is a record and an explanation of what must seem, to dwellers in less happy lands, an economic miracle. In these last years Swedish Recovery, from trade depression and mass unemployment, has been sensational. External factors, such as the rise in certain export prices, have helped a little. But primarily the Recovery is due to internal action, based largely on the theories of Gunnar Myrdal, and executed with great political skill and economic insight by Ernst Wigforss, the brilliant Finance Minister in the Swedish Socialist Government led by Per Albin Hansson. In this action, monetary and budgetary policy have been closely linked. And for this purpose it has been of fundamental importance that in Sweden the Central Bank is publicly owned and under the direct control of the Government and Parliament. The very rapid fall in unemployment has resulted from a bold programme of increased investment, particularly in public enterprises. These play an important role in the Swedish national economy, which is considerably more socialist than ours. Thus

" public works " is a phrase of much wider meaning in Sweden than with us, and covers operations of a much more varied and productive character.

The budget statement for 1936–7 is a remarkable vindication of this policy. A substantial surplus is anticipated; a mass of short term debts is to be paid off; further public investment on a large scale is provided for, to be financed partly by loan and partly from revenue; and a reduction of income tax is announced, while the increase in the death duties, imposed two years ago to cover the service of the short term debts now to be repaid, is retained. Swedish practice is in harmony with the more hopeful and constructive economic theories of the present day. We can learn much from it, through this book.

HUGH DALTON.

LONDON SCHOOL OF ECONOMICS.
February, 1936.

INTRODUCTION

MONETARY policy is interpreted in this book in the broadest sense, for there is no English word which conveys the meaning of the useful foreign term *Konjunkturpolitik*. This denotes a combination of credit, budgetary, commercial, and wage policies aimed at smoothing out industrial fluctuations. The analysis presented in this book is based on the theory and practice evolved in one particular country.

Sweden has a population of slightly over six millions which is about three-quarters of the size of Greater London. Relatively to the larger nations her influence on world affairs is negligible, and at first sight it might seem that the internal characteristics of so small a unit are of subordinate interest. It happens, however, that Sweden's contributions to economic science have been of a significance out of all proportion to the size of the country. Some of the most fruitful additions to pre-War economic thought are associated with the names of Knut Wicksell, Gustav Cassel, and David Davidson. The tradition has been maintained in recent years by a young group of distinguished economists who have made important advances particularly in monetary and trade cycle theory.

The world depression brought in its train a whole avalanche of controversy. Both in this country and in the United States some observers thought they detected in Sweden a bright ray of light which pierced the prevailing gloom. Professor Irving Fisher and his circle have pointed to the so-called "stabilization" policy pursued in Sweden since 1931 as a proof that "the dance of the dollar" can be brought to an end as soon as the Americans decide to emulate the Swedes. There is nothing mysterious in the recent recovery of Sweden; and certainly no one even slightly acquainted with the country's economic literature and policy would find there a justification for the gospel of price stabilization. The interesting thing is that in this small country for the last twenty years there has been an interaction of economic theory and practice. During the Great War when Sweden experienced a severe inflation as a result of the extraordinary circumstances of the time, the leading economists put their theoretical equipment at the service of the statesmen and bankers and they learnt much in the process. The second period of emergency, due to the world slump, found a new group of economists eager to prescribe on the basis of more advanced methods of diagnosis. Theoretical controversies of a notably high quality took place and a crisis policy emerged which bore the imprint of the works of the theorists.

In this book I have examined the measures adopted in Sweden to cope with the crisis due to the War and the crisis of the world slump and the bearing of theoretical speculation on these policies. I have tried to indicate the direction in which monetary and trade cycle theory has been developing in Sweden. Not the least important part of the documentation consists of the monumental volumes of the Unemployment Commission appointed in 1927. This Commission began its labours in the early stage of the pre-1929 expansion and did not present its final report until 1935, when events had completed the full circle and recovery had again begun. The Interim Report was published in 1931 under the title, *The Magnitude, Character, and Causes of Unemployment*; and the Final Report, *Measures against Unemployment*, which summarizes the economists' theoretical results and incorporates the Commission's recommendations, appeared in 1935.

The Commission adopted an interesting procedure, somewhat reminiscent of the British Royal Commission on Imperial and Local Taxation of 1898 which elicited from the leading economists of that time a series of memoranda in reply to a questionnaire on the incidence of taxation. The theoretical problems involved in a consideration of State policy to cope with unemployment were handed to the professional economists ; and the results are embodied in a series of valuable analytical studies on such themes as Wages and Unemployment, Price Movements in the Trade Cycle, the Causes of Unemployment, Industrial Rationalization and its Effects, the Economic Consequences of Public Finance Policy, Monetary Policy, Public Works, Subsidies and Tariffs as Means of dealing with Unemployment. It would be difficult to find in the official publications of any other country a parallel to this impressive achievement. Sweden has reason to be proud of the high standard of her analytical economics and of the commendable endeavour of her economists to make the science fruit-bearing.

Sweden managed to remain neutral during the World War ; but that great cataclysm had a profound effect on the country's fortunes. The economic implications of neutrality raise problems of absorbing interest, and it will be the task of this book to examine how the internal course of events was moulded by powerful outside forces. It would be a fascinating inquiry for the sociologist to trace the effects of the conflicting pulls of Anglo-Saxon and German culture on the Swedish character. The Great War revealed the existence of a powerful pro-German sentiment among the Swedes, particularly in the middle and upper classes, and it was doubtless enhanced by the enormous profits to be made by exporting vital commodities to Germany in the first two years of the struggle. But the vicissitudes of the post-War period have altered the balance. There can be no doubt that since the triumph of Nazism in Germany the sympathies of Sweden have been drawn much closer towards Great Britain. The Swede is as proud as the Britisher of his heritage of civic freedom and government by consent; and he is probably more alive to the dangers that threaten these institutions. The conditions are now present for a strengthening of the bonds of affinity between this country and the three Scandinavian kingdoms.

The economic structure of Sweden resembles that of the great industrial nations. The possession of rich supplies of iron ore and timber, a marked inventive propensity, and a well-established parliamentary constitution, made the rapid advance of industrialization inevitable in the second half of the nineteenth century. The distribution of labour as between agriculture and industry was revolutionized in the forty years before the War. In 1870 3,017,000 people or 72 per cent of the total were employed in agriculture and 872,000 or

20 per cent in industry, mining, and commerce; by 1920 the number employed in agriculture had declined to 2,596,000 or 44 per cent, while the other group had expanded to 2,964,000 or 47 per cent. This industrial revolution gave birth to a trade union system which is probably stronger than in any other European country and a Co-operative Movement which is now responsible for over one-tenth of the total retail turnover. Like its British equivalent, the Swedish Labour Party is imbued with an attitude of common-sense empiricism and is fortunately free from the barren obsession with theoretical speculation which was the bane of what was once German Social Democracy. The Bank of Sweden is publicly owned and is responsible to the Banking Committee of the Riksdag. Under the able leadership of Branting, the Swedish Party was the first in Europe to form a Labour Government. Another Labour Administration took office in September, 1932, at a time when the country was feeling the worst effects of the world depression, and it has ridden the storm with conspicuous success. It is one of the objects of this book to analyse the nature of Sweden's recovery and the bearing on it of the State's monetary and financial policy.

It is only the accident of language which has prevented Swedish economic thought from exercising a greater influence on other countries.

In the last few years economic analysis in England has been enriched by the absorption of ideas from another small country—Austria. There is, however, a northern shrine where the English-speaking pilgrim may also derive inspiration, if he is prepared to take upon himself the burden of a difficult language. Intellectual resources are put to the best use when there is free international exchange of ideas, unhindered by barriers of language. But it should be free exchange over the whole field and not confined to regional *blocs*.

The foundations of the Swedish and Austrian schools have much in common. Some of the ideas worked out in their fullness by Böhm-Bawerk are to be found in Davidson's first book published in 1878; and Wicksell's contribution to capital theory consists in a refinement of the work of Böhm-Bawerk. But the edifice which Professors Lindahl and Myrdal—to name but two representatives of the present generation of Swedish economists—are building on these foundations is of rather a different style from the structure of which the architects are Professors Mises and Hayek. Unfortunately the difficulty of language has hitherto kept most of the work of this Swedish school inaccessible to the outside world. This book will have been of some service if it succeeds in giving some broad indications of the trend of their thought.

It is interesting that in Sweden great respect

is paid to the professional economist. He commands an honoured place in the scheme of things, in marked contrast to the scepticism or the polite indifference with which he is regarded in this country and in the United States. This is the case despite the fact that university teachers and even civil servants are allowed by the rules of Swedish democratic government to take an active part in politics. The present leader of the Conservative Party—Professor Bagge—holds a chair of Economics in the University of Stockholm. Professor Myrdal, who succeeded Professor Cassel in the same University, has been for some years a prominent economic adviser of the Labour Government, and is now an elected member of the Swedish Second Chamber. Even the great Wicksell himself, one of the most austere of pure theorists, was a radical in politics. He once expressed such outspoken anti-Christian sentiments that he was actually put in prison, and the preface to one of his books bears the name of that institution. There could be no stronger evidence to show that Sweden takes her economists seriously. The curious thing is that though they often take their part in the hurly-burly of politics, the authority attaching to their pronouncements is not thereby weakened. The Swede is thoroughly democratic and regards it as axiomatic that every citizen, even though he be the servant of the State, should have an equal opportunity of taking part in the process of government.

I feel a deep sense of gratitude to a number of Swedish economists, politicians, bankers, trade union leaders, and business men, who generously allowed me to avail myself of their knowledge and experience. I owe to them the fact that in the course of six months I was able to probe beneath the surface of things and to enjoy a hospitality the memory of which I shall always cherish. In particular I wish to express my great indebtedness to Professors Gunnar Myrdal, Erik Lindahl, and Bertil Ohlin for the interest they took in my researches and for the valuable opportunity of acquainting myself with their theoretical technique.

My thanks are due to Mr. Wigforss, the Minister of Finance in the present Government, and Mr. Ivar Rooth, the Governor of the Bank of Sweden, for the privilege of approaching them with some of my problems; and to Professor Göste Bagge, Director of the Social Science Institute of the University of Stockholm, where I enjoyed excellent library facilities. I derived much benefit from discussions with Professor E. Heckscher, Dr. Johan Åkerman, Dr. D. Hammarskjöld, Dr. A. Johansson, Dr. Karin Kock, Dr. T. Palander, and Mr. I. Svennilson.

I must also express my gratitude to Sir Archibald Clark Kerr, then His Majesty's

Minister in Stockholm, through whose kindness I was able to meet prominent leaders in Swedish public life, and to my friend, Mr. T. G. Barman, *The Times* correspondent for Scandinavia, who has taught me a great deal about the Northern countries.

Dr. P. N. Rosenstein-Rodan, of University College, London, did me the service of reading Chapters II, III, and IV in manuscript and made valuable suggestions.

Finally, I owe more than I can say to the interest taken in this book by Dr. Hugh Dalton. It was he who suggested the idea originally; and he gave me the benefit of his detailed comments on every chapter.

MONETARY POLICY AND CRISES

Chapter I

INFLATION IN A NEUTRAL COUNTRY, 1914–1920

THE World Crisis divided the nations into belligerents and neutrals. In the former the problem facing the authorities was to make the greatest possible use of national resources for the purpose of waging war. One of the important consequences of this was the depreciation of currencies. Internal price structures became hopelessly distorted; the range of Governmental control widened enormously; and the international exchange of goods and services was dominated by naval warfare and blockade. All this meant revolutionary changes in the economic life of small countries which remained neutral, particularly those which had developed intimate commercial relations with the rest of the world. They found themselves at the mercy of powerful and erratic currents. They were like small tugs being towed willy-nilly by a gigantic liner through tempestuous seas. For economic and geographical reasons Sweden was profoundly affected by the War. It is proposed to examine the nature of her crisis and the manner in which the authorities sought to solve the baffling problems inflicted upon them.

(1) An Inconvertible Paper Currency

The outbreak of the War came at a time when Sweden was experiencing a reaction from the speculative boom of 1912. The immediate result was that on the 2nd August, 1914, the convertibility of the currency was suspended. The discount rate was put up to $6\frac{1}{2}$ per cent; the Stock Exchange and the banks were closed; and a general moratorium was declared until the 7th September. Sweden had suddenly been thrown on to an inconvertible paper standard. Gilt-edged bills were made eligible as supplementary note backing; and the Riksbank received the right to issue fiduciary notes up to the amount of 125 million kronor.[1]

The Governor of the Central Bank was facing an unprecedented situation; and his policy was soon to become the object of sharp criticism. Early in August, Gustav Cassel rather injudiciously rushed into print with a programme of action which he then thought would cope with the probable future course of events.[2] He was in favour of suspending convertibility,

[1] A. Wennerberg, "Sveriges Riksbank och dess diskontopolitik under och efter världskriget," *Ekonomisk Tidskrift*, 1924, p. 226.

[2] *Svenska Dagbladet*, 4th August, 1914.

a step which he thought would not be dangerous so long as the note issue was kept within reasonable limits. The only alternative, in his view, was a 10 per cent bank rate; and he stressed the advantage of maintaining the gold reserve so as to facilitate convertibility as soon as the War, which he anticipated would be short-lived, was at an end. He advised entrepreneurs to produce for stock so that they could sell out at a profit when hostilities were over. The role of a prophet is always a hazardous one. Cassel soon found it necessary to change his views; and he became the most severe critic of the Bank authorities.

The manner in which Sweden departed from the gold standard was, strictly speaking, unconstitutional, for the convertibility of notes was guaranteed by law. It was not till April, 1915, that an Amending Bill was passed; and thus, in the words of Professor Heckscher, "paper money was legitimized about nine months after its birth".[1] The note circulation, after a sharp increase from 206 million kronor on the 25th July to 282 million kronor on the 8th August, remained fairly stable until the end of 1915. But during the early months of the War the value of the krona in terms of sterling and the dollar progressively declined. Wicksell[2]

[1] Heckscher, "Monetary History, 1914–1925" in *Sweden, Norway, Denmark, and Iceland in the World War* (*Economic and Social History of the World War*, ed. by Shotwell) (1930), p. 139.

[2] "Riksbankens guldkassa," *E.T.*, 1914, p. 263.

and Heckscher [1] severely attacked the Bank for its superstitious anxiety to maintain the gold reserve. Wicksell boldly declared that "economically we could do nothing better than exchange our barren reserve of 100 million kronor of metal for useful goods from abroad." [2]

One of the motives of the Bank in allowing the exchange to depreciate was to avoid undue losses on its holdings of 100 million kronor in German bills. If the krona had remained at par the Bank would have had to bear the full brunt of the depreciation of the German mark; and the loss in selling its mark holdings would have wiped out its ordinary profit. Governor Moll, in defending his policy, actually stressed the loss to the revenue which this would have involved.[3] It must be remembered, however, that the Riksbank is a State-owned institution responsible to Parliament, and this episode illustrates the complications which can arise when the Central Bank is the servant of the Legislature. The economists made it clear that the Bank was simply making the public foot the bill by diminishing the value of money by about 7 per cent.

The belligerent countries soon discovered that the worship of the "golden calf" was incompatible with the business of effectively waging war. The neutral countries began to

[1] *Världkrigets ekonomi* (1915), p. 102.
[2] Loc. cit., p. 263.
[3] See V. Moll, "Växelkurs ock bankränta," *E.T.*, 1915, No. 6.

receive considerable gold shipments. During the first sixteen months of the War the gold reserve of the Bank of Sweden increased only from 105 to 113 million kronor; but from the 4th December, 1915, to the 5th February, 1916, it rose by no less than 50 million kronor. Meanwhile the external value of the currency in terms of sterling had not only returned to par, but at the end of 1915 was actually rising. The Central Bank was faced with quite a new problem. There were no price statistics available at that time, so that monetary management to maintain the internal value of the currency was exceedingly difficult. In the new circumstances the maintenance of a constant ratio between the gold reserve and the note circulation obviously could not prevent inflation.

The proportion of the gold reserve to the note circulation in the years 1914–17 was as follows[1]:—

Gold Reserve as Percentage of Note Circulation

	Highest.	*Lowest.*	*Average.*
1914 . .	53	35	42
1915 . .	43	36	40
1916 . .	56	41	49
1917 . .	52	41	45

Professor Davidson wrote an article at the end of 1915 in which he showed that in the existing situation Sweden could do nothing but keep the value of its currency on a level

[1] See Davidson, "Riksbanken och penningens värde under kristiden," *E.T.*, 1925.

with gold[1]; but this meant joining in the general inflation. He hinted that it would be quite otherwise, if the obligation of the Bank to buy gold at a fixed price were abolished. Then the Central Bank could exercise an influence on the value of the currency. This was the immediate origin of the well-known policy of gold exclusion. Early in 1916 Moll, the Governor of the Riksbank, communicated privately with the three leading economists, Wicksell, Davidson, and Cassel, asking them for their considered opinion on such a step.[2] The replies were favourable; and the experiment came into operation in February, 1916. It was thus made possible for the Swedish currency to rise in value, while its lower limit would be determined by the value of gold, since notes were again to be redeemable.

The first phase of Sweden's war experience came to a close with the inauguration of this bold experiment. Price index numbers, worked out retrospectively, show that in 1915 the wholesale price level rose from 135 (first quarter) to 155 (fourth quarter).[3] The volume of output in the chief branches of production also advanced considerably. The stage was being set for an inflation which was to reach

[1] "Till frågan om penningens värde under kriget," *E.T.*, 1915, pp. 415–423.

[2] See G. Cassel, *Money and Foreign Exchange after 1914* (1922), pp. 72–100.

[3] The index compiled by *Svenska Handelstidningen*.

extreme heights in the years 1917 and 1918. The phenomena in this process call for close examination. They have an added interest, in that Sweden's distinguished economists took great pains in seeking to elucidate the factors at work.

(2) Gold Exclusion

It is curious how the Bank of Sweden in deciding on policies which had profound economic significance seems to have been largely guided by considerations of its own banking interests. The rapid inflow of gold early in 1916 prompted the Bank to address a memorandum to the Government, in which it said, " The present rates on the exchange market make it impossible for the Bank to dispose of such gold as is not required for its own needs without very considerable loss." Its action immediately after gold exclusion had been introduced proved that it was completely out of sympathy with the aims of the economists. The discount rate was reduced from 5½ per cent to 5 per cent on the 1st May, 1916. If the new experiment was to be a potent factor in raising the internal value of the currency, or preventing a further deterioration, it was the duty of the Central Bank to stiffen credit conditions. There was, moreover, another serious obstacle. The terms of the

Scandinavian Monetary Union enabled Denmark and Norway to export gold coins into Sweden, where they had to be accepted at par. That this had a serious effect is shown by the following table [1] :—

HOLDINGS OF GOLD COINS (MILLION KRONOR.)

	Swedish Riksbank.	*Bank of Norway.*	*Bank of Denmark.*
31st December, 1913 .	55·96	40·74	18·21
31st December, 1914 .	55·42	35·44	34·45
31st December, 1915 .	55·44	42·92	32·34
31st December, 1916 .	73·23	41·91	26·49
31st December, 1917 .	109·67	22·92	17·89

It was not to the interest of Denmark and Norway to raise the value of their currencies above that of gold; they went on importing the metal and could send it to Sweden in a minted form. Towards the end of 1916 Davidson, at the request of the Riksbank, drew up a memorandum in which he advocated the deletion of the clause in the Scandinavian Monetary Convention which made the coinage legal tender in all three countries. The Bank then urged the Government to take steps to achieve this end. Finally after long negotiations, the three Governments agreed in April, 1917, to enforce a rigid prohibition of gold exports.

(3) STATE EXPENDITURE

The budget figures for the inflation period cannot be taken as they stand owing to the

[1] See D. Davidson, "Spridda studier angående prisstegringen," *E.T.*, 1918.

exigencies of War-time finance. As soon as war breaks out, all non-belligerent countries are immediately forced to incur new expenditure in order to safeguard their neutrality. In the first two years of the War this was responsible for most of the addition to the Swedish expenditure account. But the actual burden was not borne at the time. The costs of neutrality in the first year were defrayed out of a special credit of 50 million kronor and it was only later, when the actual outlay was known, that they were brought into the ordinary budget. Thus the Riksdag of 1915 inserted the neutrality costs of 1914 in the budget for 1916 : similarly the 1915 costs appeared in the 1917 budget. The same was true to some extent of the State grants to alleviate the incidence of the high cost of living on the poorer classes. This practice was of doubtful wisdom and it seriously aggravated the budgetary situation in 1918.

The early stage of the inflation was not much influenced by the needs of the Treasury for increased purchasing-power. But the years 1917 and 1918 saw an enormous extension of State regulation of the economic system. Three important Commissions—for food, fuel, and industry—developed a huge appetite for floating capital. Instead of paying a high rate of interest by incurring funded debt, the Government financed these Commissions with short-term loans. So the floating debt in 1918 soared to a height of 559 million kronor compared with a mere 20 million kronor before the War. This had a disturbing effect on the national finances. Critics of the Government, particularly Professor Cassel, seized on this policy as one of the chief causes of the expansion of the note issue and of the internal depreciation of the currency. The Finance Ministry's intention was that, if any losses were incurred by the Commissions, they should be met by estimates under ordinary expenditure. The Riksdag in 1917 and 1918 voted credits to the amount of 435 million kronor for the three Commissions, and the Public Debt Office resorted to the Riksbank. Finally an arrangement had to be made whereby a consortium of twenty-three banks gave the Commissions a credit of 550 million kronor, 225 million of which were to be devoted to repayment of debts to the Public Debt Office. This made very little difference in practice. Increased borrowing by the State, whether directly done through the private banks or the Riksbank, was bound to mean an expansion in the volume of circulation unless measures were taken to restrict private credits correspondingly. The major part of the losses on the Fuel and Industry Commissions was not covered in the ordinary budget, but was included in the capital account. But this was not capital expenditure in the sense of an addition to national income-yielding assets. It was bad budgetary practice. Where the service of these credits necessitated the use of other revenues, it should have been regarded as an addition to the ordinary expenditure of the period in question. Estimates in the capital account, financed by short-term loans which were later repaid, should not have been included in that account.

When allowance is made for War-time financial practices and the proper income and expenditure is imputed to each financial year, we arrive at a result somewhat different from the closed accounts of the Finance Ministry. The following table is a corrected statement.

CORRECTED STATEMENT OF ORDINARY AND CAPITAL EXPENDITURE IN SWEDEN, 1913–1922.[1] (IN MILLION KRONOR)

Financial Year.	*Ordinary Expenditure.*	*Capital Expenditure.*	*Total.*
1913 . .	204·6	60·7	265·3
1914 . .	270·4	58·9	329·3
1915 . .	347·9	58·5	406·4
1916 . .	384·1	64·5	448·6
1917 . .	471·5	91·8	563·3
1918 . .	897·4	176·7	1074·1
1919 . .	674·5	175·1	849·6
1920 . .	758·5	193·3	951·8
1921 . .	825·9	258·6	1084·1
1922 . .	769·9	140·0	909·1

The increases in 1915 and 1916 were mainly caused by national defence requirements. The financial year 1917 was burdened by abnormal expenses connected with allowances for the

[1] Erik Stridsberg, " Statsbudgeten under och efter kristiden," *Nationalekonomiska Föreningens Förhandlingar*, 1925, p. 4.

high cost of living, e.g. grants to public officials and the provision of working capital for the special Commissions. The sharp jump in 1918 is partly explained by the fall in the value of money. Administrative costs were swollen and the provision for unemployment relief and measures for regulating the prices of foodstuffs in the interests of the poor were introduced. Moreover an item of 102·5 million kronor in 1918 is accounted for by the losses on the Fuel and Industry Commissions and the current deficit on the State Railways. The disappearance of some of these extraordinary War-time items explains the contraction of ordinary expenditure in 1919.

The conduct of the national finances in the first three years of the War did much to aggravate the inflation of 1917–18. In the financial year 1916 the surplus shown in the closed accounts was 91·4 millions and the Treasury's cash balance was 127·9 millions. The year 1917 gave a surplus of 247 millions and the cash balance grew to 375 millions. But current revenue had by no means borne the cost of current expenditure. The Riksdag, alarmed by the progressive deterioration of the currency, adopted a new principle in 1917, according to which the expenditure within the financial year must be covered by the revenue of that year. The items of expenditure to be incurred up to the end of 1918, but for which no cover had been provided, were to be put in a supplementary budget.[1] The total expenditure in this special budget was 660·9 million kronor, of which 233·9 million were on current, and 436·9 million on capital account. 398·5 million of the cover were obtained by realizing capital assets and the rest by borrowing and using the cash reserve. The estimates for 1918 thus rose sharply: provision had to be made for two years' neutrality costs, large votes for the alleviation of the high cost of living for the poor, and credits for the special Commissions.[2] If the budget had been more rationally balanced in the early years of the War, the demands of the State in the year 1918 would have been less burdensome. As it was, a large extension of public borrowing had to be made at the very time when the other factors at the root of the inflation were exercising their strongest influence.

(4) The Inadequacy of Gold Exclusion

One of the most puzzling features of the Swedish situation was the co-existence of a considerable rise in the price level, relatively to that of England and the United States, with a depreciation of the currencies of those countries in terms of the Swedish krona.

[1] Karl Hildebrand, *De svenska statsmakterna och krigstidens folkhushållning*, 1918, pp. 26–7.

[2] Ibid., p. 26.

Diagram III shows that between the second quarter of 1917 and the third quarter of 1918 the Swedish price level, expressed as a percentage of the British, moved from 108 to 150, whereas sterling fell in value in terms of the krona from 87 to 75. The explanation of this phenomenon depends on our interpretation of the abnormal circumstances of the time.

We have seen that gold exclusion was introduced in the first instance to free the Central Bank from the embarrassment of the gold influx. After the agreement with Norway and Denmark in April, 1917, the embargo could be made effective; and this factor making for internal depreciation lost its potency. But, strangely enough, the Bank continued to purchase gold, as is clear from the following table [1]:—

GOLD IMPORTS, 1915–17. (IN MILLION KRONOR)

	In Scandinavian Currency.	*Gold in Other Forms.*	*Total.*
Years 1915–17 . .	59·11	81·57	140·68
From the introduction of Gold Exclusion in February, 1916, to end of 1917 . . .	59·00	29·80	88·80
August, 1917, to end of 1917 . . .	24·07	16·29	40·36

There is no reason to think that Denmark and Norway did not keep the terms of the

[1] Heckscher, *Penningväsende och penningpolitik*, 1914–1925, p. 70, in *Bidrag till Sveriges ekonomiska och sociala historia under och efter världskriget* (ed. by E. Heckscher, 1926).

Agreement of April, 1917. We must therefore conclude that the Riksbank had new reasons for voluntarily acquiring gold, even though the relative improvement in the exchange value of the krona made it more expensive. We can only surmise that the Bank authorities had by that time changed their attitude and were now anxious to strengthen the gold reserve as a basis for an expansion of the note issue. The conclusion seems to be that the Bank not only refused to see in the gold exclusion policy an instrument for protecting the internal value of the currency, but also abandoned even its own original motive for keeping out gold. In spite of the apparent contradictions in official policy, there is no doubt that gold exclusion did contribute something towards curbing internal inflation. It was an interesting attempt to implement an idea which was known only to a few theorists on the eve of the War. That it was not very effective was due to a complex of other factors. Among these we may mention the insatiable demand for Swedish exports which led to an abnormal volume of foreign credits, a faulty bank rate policy, the huge growth in public expenditure, the influence of physical scarcity of commodities, and business speculation.

(5) The Foreign Trade Situation

During the first two years of the War the Swedish Government made strenuous attempts to defend its interests as a neutral country against what it considered to be gross infringement of international law by the belligerent Powers.[1] But its efforts were in vain. The operation of the British blockade, which implied such measures as the extortion of guarantees against the re-export of imports, bunker coal contracts, and black lists, was a serious interference with Sweden's control over her own trade. The declaration of unrestricted submarine warfare by Germany in the spring of 1917 and the entry of the United States into the War gave Sweden no option but to secure the provision of vital imports by granting large concessions to both sides. The geographical situation of the country made it inevitable that the export and re-export trade with Germany would play an important part; and in the early part of the War this led to a considerable boom.[2] The following table [3] gives the course of the prices of important export goods compared with that of the general price indices up to the end of 1916.

[1] See K. Bergendal, *Handels- och sjöfartspolitik under världskriget* in *Bidrag till Sveriges ekonomiska och sociala historia....*

[2] See Kurt Bergendal, op. cit., and *Affärsvärlden*, 1916, *passim.*

[3] Heckscher, op. cit., pp. 39, 47, and 81.

	1914. I.	II.	1915 (Quarters). I.	II.	III.	IV.	1916. I.	II.	III.	IV
Swedish wholesale prices [1]	111	120	135	143	147	155	164	175	191	209
British wholesale prices [1]	106	108	120	128	128	136	152	160	159	178
Export pig iron (in Swedish currency) [2] .	104	104	111	131	143	179	193	215	248	359
Mechanical pulp (in Swedish currency) [2] .	111	111	115	118	126	131	158	204	253	268
Chemical pulp (in Swedish currency) [2] .	112	104	101	104	126	148	184	254	287	283

The rise in export prices in 1915 was caused chiefly by German demand. "As against 1914 the rise of exports (in 1915) over that of imports had increased in the case of Germany by 298,600,000 kronor compared with only 41,500,000 kronor for Britain. And it is natural to feel that there was such a tendency from the outbreak of the War." [3] It is little wonder that the organizers of the blockade turned their earnest attention to the Baltic; and from 1916 onwards it became increasingly difficult for Germany to receive supplies from Sweden. Colossal material destruction implied a growing scarcity of goods. The prices of Swedish export goods soared to unprecedented heights in 1917 and 1918, as the continuation of our table on p. 18 brings out.

The abnormal conditions of demand for Swedish exports had a great deal to do with the character of the inflation. Professor Heckscher calculates the net export of capital

[1] July 1913–June 1914 = 100. [2] January–July 1914 = 100.

[3] Heckscher, in *Sweden, Denmark, Norway and Iceland in the World War*, pp. 168–9. For a vigorous exposure of the extent to which Germany was able to procure essential supplies through Scandinavia, see *The Triumph of Unarmed Forces* (1923), by Rear-Admiral M. W. P. Consett, who was naval attaché in Scandinavia 1912–19.

	1917 (quarters)				1918.			
	I.	II.	III.	IV.	I.	II.	III.	IV.
Swedish wholesale prices .	225	229	249	272	305	331	351	370
British wholesale prices .	197	212	211	219	224	229	234	235
Export pig iron (in Swedish currency)	410	378	428	421	(418)	(403)	(387)	(384)[1]
Mechanical pulp (in Swedish currency)	275	293	299	299	363	403	401	400
Chemical pulp (in Swedish currency)	283	279	264	256	259	264	274	297

in 1916 at a figure of 670 million kronor.[2] Sweden placed its credit at the disposal of foreign countries in various ways of which a rough statistical estimate for 1916 can be given.[3] The import of securities from abroad amounted to about 185 million kronor; the accumulation of the assets of Swedish banks in foreign countries accounted for 300 millions; and 60 million kronor of gold were imported. According to these figures direct credits granted through exporters made up only about 19 per cent of the total. As the demand for Swedish products became more and more intense in 1917 and 1918, the role played by foreign credits became more important. This was a powerful cause of internal inflation which could not be nullified merely by keeping the money rate of interest "normal" in relation to the yield of internal investment.

In 1917 the stringency of the British blockade severely curtailed Swedish imports, but did not have such a drastic effect on exports. The value of imports in that year was only 56 per

[1] For 1918 the export pig iron prices are available only for four months. The figures in the table are based on home market prices.

[2] See Heckscher, *Penningväsende och penningpolitik*, p. 75.

[3] Ibid., p. 91.

cent of the value of exports; the excess of exports amounted to no less than 591 million kronor. Net capital exports in 1917 work out at 760 million kronor, a smaller total than in the previous year if the change in the value of money is allowed for. Nevertheless it was a considerable volume for a country which, as Professor Heckscher pointed out, was living to a great extent under a blockade. During 1918 the import situation eased and the revenue from shipping improved. The value of the export surplus thus declined to 460 million kronor which in real terms was only about one-third of the corresponding amount in 1916.

(6) Production, Prices and Wages

After the initial dislocation due to the shock of the outbreak of War, production and foreign trade proceeded fairly smoothly for the first two years. The demand for the country's products had greatly increased and for the time being the obstacles impeding the supply of raw materials and other imports were not considerable. During this first phase the volume of output in such trades as textiles, clothing, leather, hair, rubber, and chemicals showed a substantial advance relatively to industry as a whole. But the year 1916 already showed signs of an unhealthy boom. The average value of the industrial production of capital goods in that year was double what it was in 1913, whereas the corresponding index for consumers' goods rose by only 60 per cent. Investment had become very profitable and the optimistic anticipations of producers were already causing capital values and commodity prices to rise. As we have already seen, this was the period when gold imports were also influencing the Swedish price level: a restrictive credit policy would not have sufficed to prevent a boom.

In the years 1917 and 1918 the position became much more complicated. The index number of the *value* of the industrial output of capital goods went up to 294 and 327 respectively; but the corresponding consumers' goods index actually fell in 1917 to 160 and advanced only very slightly in the following year. The precipitous upward course of the wholesale price level was steeper than that of the note circulation. The weighted index numbers of the average price of exports registered 224 and 400 in these two years, while import prices reached a level of 256 and 314 respectively. The index of the general volume of production fell from 109 in 1916 to 76 in 1918, a decline which was by no means uniform over different trades. The output in mining and metal, wood, paper, and pulp industries, decreased less than the average, while food, textiles, and clothing suffered a diminution of output much more severe than industry as a whole. A feverish inflation was combined with substantial decline in physical production,[1] and this entailed a fall in the average physical productivity of labour in different industries.

The terms of trade, which had been unfavourable to Sweden in 1915, became favourable in the years 1916–18. The course of the price indices of imports and exports are given in the following table :—

PRICE LEVEL OF IMPORTS AND EXPORTS [2]

1913 = 100

	Imports (weighted).	Exports (weighted).
1915 . .	135	139
1916 . .	158	190
1917 . .	224	256
1918 . .	400	314
1919 . .	329	298
1920 . .	338	317
1921 . .	191	222
1922 . .	141	157
1923 . .	130	160

In interpreting these figures it must be remembered that the price of imports was influenced by the abnormally high freight rates during the latter part of the War.[3] Moreover the physical export surplus of 1916, 1917, and

[1] Compare the experience of Germany in 1923, see Bresciani-Turroni, *Le Vicende del Marco Tedesco* (1931).

[2] Edström in *Sweden, Denmark, Norway, and Iceland in the World War*, p. 242.

[3] This factor is also important in its bearing on exchange rates.

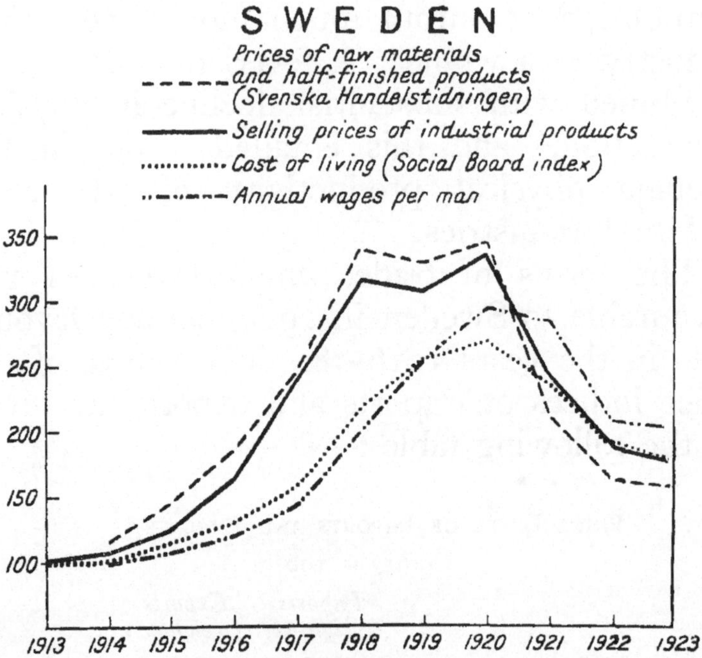

DIAGRAM 1.

	Prices of raw materials and half-finished products (Svenska Handelstidningen).	*Selling prices of industrial products.*	*Cost of living (Social Board Index).*	*Annual wages per man.*
	July, 1913–June, 1914=100	1913=100	1914=100	1913=100
1914 . .	116	104	100	100
1915 . .	145	122	115	107
1916 . .	185	164	130	120
1917 . .	244	237	159	143
1918 . .	339	317	219	200
1919 . .	330	308	257	256
1920 . .	347	335	270	294
1921 . .	211	242	236	271
1922 . .	162	188	190	208
1923 . .	157	176	174	202

Olaf Edström in *Bidrag till Sveriges ekonomiska och sociala historia under och efter världskriget* (edited by Professor E. Heckscher, 1926), pp. 236 and 239.

early 1918 was partially liquidated in goods immediately after the War in 1918–19 when the price level of imports was much higher than that of exports. Sweden had thus to accept a smaller quantity of imports in exchange for her exports.

An interesting aspect of the inflationary process is illuminated by Diagram I, which gives the course of the average selling price of industrial products, the price level of raw materials and half-finished goods, and the annual wage level. The value of raw materials and other intermediate products rose faster than that of industrial products ; but the annual wage level lagged very far behind. The price of labour to employers was relatively low even allowing for the falling off in efficiency. Wages rose almost as fast as the cost of living ; but it is surprising that the competition of employers did not raise wages higher. At the end of 1916 the workers' representatives met in a " cost of living conference " in Stockholm and protested against the progressive fall in real wages. They admitted that, in so far as high prices were due to scarcity of goods, real wages could be expected to fall correspondingly. But there were other causes of the rising price level and they insisted that the workers should not have to bear an unjust burden. The State interfered to ration foodstuffs and thereby regulate their prices ; but the full implications of its policy were not realized at the time. There is no doubt that the Government's policy was a stimulus to the process of inflation. The conditions of demand for capital goods and intermediate products (e.g. iron, metal goods) were peculiarly favourable owing to the urgent requirements of the belligerent powers. The State, by holding the price of foodstuffs relatively low, was really giving the entrepreneurs in the higher stages of production who had their eye on the foreign market a subsidy in the form of relatively cheap labour. This was almost literally the case, for during the period 1917–19 the Riksdag voted a total sum of 170 million kronor for the purpose of cheapening the more important kinds of foods.[1]

The Swedish Government, in pursuing the laudable end of preventing the hardship which the free working of the price mechanism would have inflicted upon the poorer sections of the population, was actually aggravating the problem of setting more reasonable limits to the inflation. If the prices of foodstuffs had been allowed to rise further and wages had increased more rapidly, there would have been two advantageous results : the profitability and output of agriculture and of home consumption industries would have improved and less labour would have moved into the production of

[1] See *Detaljpriser och indexberäkningar*, 1913–1930 (*Socialstyrelsen*, Official publications, 1933), p. 38.

industrial capital goods; while the rise in wages costs in the capital industries would have reduced the profit margins, speculation would have been less, and the boom would not have reached such heights. The objection might be raised that, as the belligerents' demand was very inelastic, the course of events would not have been appreciably influenced. But even so, it is hard to deny that, if wages had increased more rapidly in the early stages of the boom, the efficacy of a relatively high bank rate would have been much greater. The Governor of the Bank always emphasized that the loan rate of interest had lost its significance owing to the enormous prospects of profit; there would have been much less to be said for the official attitude if these entrepreneurs had also had to face higher wage costs.

(7) The Banks and the Speculative Boom

The speculative spirit dominated the Stock Exchange and the capital market in the years 1916–1920. The turnover of stocks and shares on the Stockholm Stock Exchange rose from a quarterly average of 45 million kronor in 1913 to 397 million in 1918. Allowing for the change in the value of money as reflected in the general price level, we get a figure of 116 million kronor for 1918. The nominal amount of capital issues for new companies increased from 106·1 million kronor in 1913 to 597·6 million in 1918: the corresponding figures for capital issues by existing companies were 111·5 million and 786·8 million respectively.

During 1915 and the first half of 1916 the banks exercised caution in the granting of credits, for they expected the War to be short-lived. The entrepreneurs, in turn, were content for the most part to utilize the existing productive apparatus to the fullest capacity, since they did not expect the higher prices to last long. In deciding on the character of his investment an entrepreneur is influenced by anticipations of a twofold character—the expected price of his product in relation to his future costs and the period for which he can expect that price to be maintained. In the latter half of 1916 and early 1917 it became clear that the War was going to be a grim, long-drawn-out struggle which would be decided as much by economic power as by military strategy. For the neutral countries this meant that the producers revised their price anticipations; they believed that the curve of their proceeds would go progressively upwards. In Sweden it was generally expected that this happy state of affairs would continue even when the War did come to an end, because the physical destruction would have been so enormous that there would still be a great demand for Sweden's export goods.

The bankers and some of the economists were by no means immune from this illusion. Undertakings were reorganized and amalgamated on a new capital basis, the depreciation of the currency having automatically reduced the burden of their fixed debt charges, new flotations became numerous, and the banks cheerfully financed these investments not only by lending liberally against the shares of the enterprises but also by granting direct credits to them.[1] Many banks even went further and formed subsidiary " investment companies " which made them directly interested in the flotation of new concerns and the extension of old ones. This was to have disastrous effects on their liquidity when the artificial stimulus to expansion had passed. It may be mentioned in this connection that, when investment takes place through the medium of subsidiary agencies owned by banks, the relationship between the " money rate " and the " natural rate " can have no bearing on the situation. The idea of the equilibrating function of a " normal " rate of interest presupposes two independent parties buying and selling credit. In a system where most of the investment was done by companies owned or controlled by the banks, the mechanism of the natural-money rate would have lost all meaning.

[1] See 1924 Banking Committee Report, *Betänkande med förslag till lag om ändring i vissa delar av lagen den 22 Juni 1911 om bankrörelse* (Official Publications, 1927), pp. 54–6.

Statistical evidence of some of the consequences of the banks' policy during the boom may be found in the 1924 Banking Committee's Report. This divides industrial concerns into three categories: namely, those which have no bank debts, or only very small ones so that they are quite independent, and can easily get further credit from any bank; and, secondly, concerns which are substantially indebted to the banks, but not to the extent of making the bank the virtual owner. In this case the company is usually unable to obtain credit from any other source. The third group includes firms whose debts are so large in relation to their assets, that the bank is virtually the owner. This usually involves a certain amount of control by the bank over the company's operations. The Committee collected figures showing the distribution of firms in different lines of production over these three categories in 1913, 1918, and 1924. The results may be summarized in the following table.

In Million Kronor

		Category I.		*Category II.*		*Category III.*	
	Total number of companies.	*Own capital.*	*Bank credit.*	*Own capital.*	*Bank credit.*	*Own capital.*	*Bank credit.*
1913 . .	492	1,246	246	20	50	22	34
1918 . .	704	3,017	665	104	136	27	54
1924 . .	693	2,594	328	200	167	454	685

After the collapse of the boom the banks found themselves saddled with numerous enterprises falling into the third category. Of the 1924 sample covering 3,248 million kronor of "own capital", no less than 454 million or almost one-seventh belonged to companies whose liabilities were so large that they were left in the hands of the banks. The practices that had led to such a situation were severely criticized by the Committee and drastic amendments to the existing Bank Law were proposed. It will be shown in a later chapter how the machinery of inspection was strengthened and to what extent the banks acted with more caution in the period 1924–1930. Swedish public opinion insisted that the freedom of the banks must be curtailed, and the Act which came into force on 1st January, 1934, is a new charter summing up the practice of the post-War period and rigidly defining the narrower sphere to which the banks' operations are henceforth to be confined.

(8) The Post-War Deflation

The peak reached by the wholesale price level in Sweden, taking 1913 as base, was 366 in June, 1920, compared with 347 in the United Kingdom in July and 279 in the United States in May. By the end of 1921 the Swedish and British indices stood at 172 and 171 respectively, while the American had fallen to 149. The extreme severity of the deflation in Sweden is partly explained by the nature of her inflation. As soon as the abnormal demand for her exports

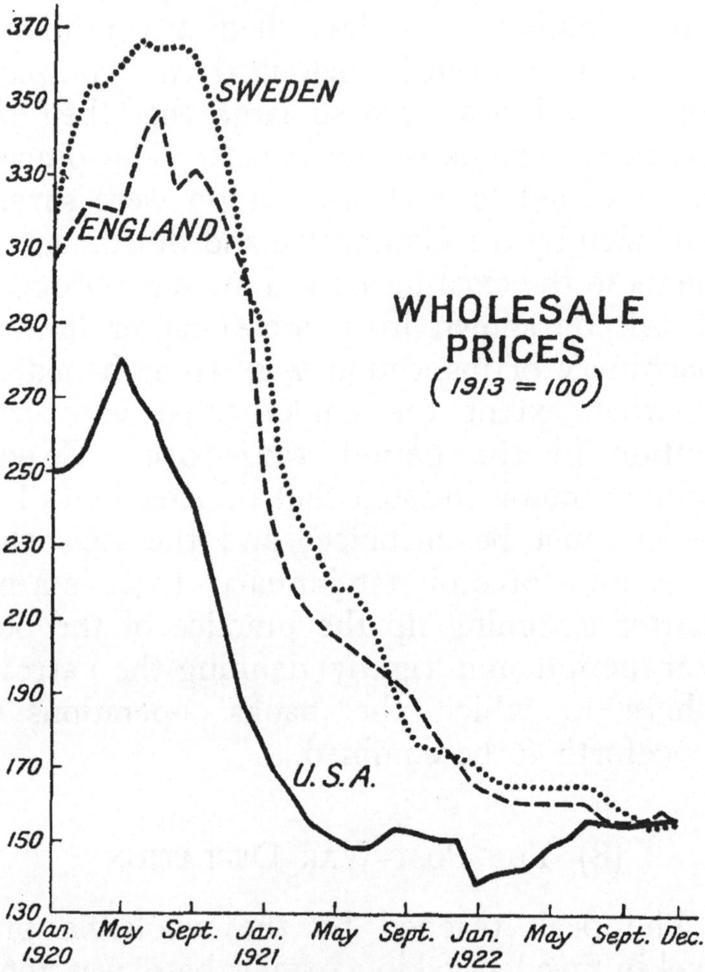

DIAGRAM 2.

THE FALL OF WHOLESALE PRICES IN SWEDEN, ENGLAND, AND U.S.A. (1913=100).

	Sweden.			*England.*			*U.S.A.*		
	1920.	*1921.*	*1922.*	*1920.*	*1921.*	*1922.*	*1920.*	*1921.*	*1922.*
January . .	319	267	170	306	251	164	248	178	138
February .	342	250	166	316	229	162	249	167	141
March . .	354	237	164	332	215	160	253	162	142
April . .	354	229	165	321	209	160	265	154	143
May . .	361	218	164	319	205	160	279	151	148
June . .	366	218	164	338	202	160	269	148	150
July . .	363	211	165	347	198	160	262	148	155
August . .	265	198	163	326	194	156	250	152	155
September .	362	182	158	331	191	154	242	152	153
October . .	346	175	155	324	184	155	225	150	154
November .	331	174	154	313	176	157	207	149	156
December .	299	172	155	302	171	155	189	149	156

disappeared and the cessation of hostilities removed the obstacles to imports, the balance in her commodity trade was reversed. No measures were taken to check the purchases from abroad, with the result that the import surplus in 1919 and 1920 was 958 and 1,036 million kronor respectively. Sweden became the victim of exchange dumping by continental countries with very depreciated currencies.

The average value of shares on the Stockholm Stock Exchange fell from 376 per cent of par in April, 1917, to 77 per cent in March, 1922. The end of the War knocked the bottom out of the Swedish boom. Between 1920 and 1922 the average price of industrial products declined from 356 to 200, and annual earnings per worker in manufacturing and mining from 278 to 186.[1] The catastrophic slump in capital values was all the more dangerous because the banks had been lending liberally against shares. Bank loans on the security of shares in proportion to the share capital of the borrowing companies amounted to 27 per cent in 1916 and in 1919 compared with 23 per cent in 1912.[2] It is estimated that the volume of loans of this kind in 1920 was 1,855 million kronor or 39 per cent of the total of loans. Most of the investment companies, which had been so

[1] I. Svennilson, *Wages in Sweden 1860–1930* (1935), part ii, p. 241.

[2] E. Heckscher, *Forhandlingar ved det Nordiske nationaløkonomiske møte* (Oslo), 1923, p. 153.

prosperous during the War, collapsed, and the banks had to write off no less than 700 million kronor. Capital values fell far more than the price level because they had been based on war-time expectations and the real burden of the companies' debts could not be adjusted when the value of money rose. The deflation was also accentuated because the rate of interest was kept comparatively high in Sweden for some time after the down-turn. It was not until April, 1921, that the discount rate was reduced from 7½ to 7 per cent; by July, 1922, it had reached 4½ per cent. This policy ensured a thorough process of liquidation; and the price level in 1922 continued to decline until by the end of that year it was only 55 per cent above 1913. In contrast to this, wholesale prices in the United States touched their lowest point in January, 1922, and then rose to 156 by the end of the year. It is interesting to note that in December, 1922, after all their divergencies, wholesale prices in Sweden, the United States, and the United Kingdom stood together at 55 per cent above 1913. But it would be quite wrong to infer from this uniformity that the process of adjustment was similar in the three countries. The inflationary experience of Sweden differed in many ways from that of the United States and the United Kingdom.

The War had a far more disturbing effect on

neutral Sweden than on the United States, though the latter country was a belligerent for two years. Both emerged from the crisis in a stronger economic position relatively to other countries. But, before Sweden could settle down again, she had to readapt her sadly distorted economic system to peacetime conditions. It was a longer and more painful process than in the United States.

Did Sweden gain more than she lost as a result of the War? Her losses due to physical destruction of property, blockade, and confiscation were negligible compared with those of the belligerent countries. Sir Josiah Stamp estimated that the civilians' income-yielding property in the European countries engaged in the War (excluding Russia) was 55,000 million pounds in 1914. "The annual growth of this property was probably between 1 and 2 per cent. On this very rough basis it appears that the War destroyed two, three, or four years' normal growth of the property of these nations, or one part in about thirty of its whole value." [1] Much of the savings of neutral countries was absorbed by the combatant nations. Sweden might have made substantial gains if she could have exchanged a large part of her money claims for real assets of permanent value in the war-making countries. But this policy led to a

[1] A. L. Bowley, *Some Economic Consequences of the Great War*, p. 88.

total loss in the case of the liabilities incurred by Russia.

The most important consequence of the War for Sweden was that she ceased to be a borrower and became a capital exporting country. She provided goods and services for foreign nations in exchange for claims maturing in the future. It is estimated that between 1914 and 1918 Swedish capital exports of all kinds amounted to at least 2,600 million kronor, a figure which excludes the surplus on transactions other than physical exports and shipping.[1] In the two years immediately after the War there was an import surplus of 1,300 million kronor; but as the value of money in those years had fallen very low, Sweden received much less than the equivalent of the services she had rendered. On the other hand, a substantial advantage was gained through the repayment of debts owed to foreigners. Securities of the value of 814 million kronor were imported during the years 1914–1925, and of these 700 million were Swedish bonds. By the end of 1921 over 80 per cent of the Swedish State bonds were in the hands of Swedish citizens compared with 8 per cent before the War. Since a considerable quantity of these securities, namely 487 millions, were repurchased in 1920, the country managed to pay off most of its past debts in sums repre-

[1] See Heckscher, *Inledande översikt*, p. 21, in *Bidrag till Sveriges ekonomiska och sociala historia*.

senting much less than the original real value. The following table shows the effects of the War on the national debt in Sweden and the United Kingdom.

Public Debts of Sweden and United Kingdom[1] (Reduced to Sterling at Average Rates of Exchange) Per Capita of Population

		Year 1913–14.	*1924 Actual.*	*Equivalent at Pre-War Values.*
Sweden :	Domestic . .	1	14	8
	Foreign . .	5	3	2
United Kingdom :	Domestic	15	147	88
	Foreign .	—	25	15

These figures reveal how much more significant the public debt is in the United Kingdom than it is in Sweden.

The change in Sweden's status in the world's capital markets caused the rate of interest to fall. Before the War the yield on Swedish Government securities had always been appreciably higher than the yield on Consols : the two rates in 1920 were 7·0 and 5·32 per cent respectively.[2] But after 1922 there was very little difference between the long-term rate in the two countries.

It is difficult to assess the quantitative importance of the above-mentioned factors. On balance there can be little doubt that Sweden's economic strength increased relatively

[1] A. L. Bowley, op. cit., p. 120. International debts arising from the War and Reparations and debts due to the countries are not included.

[2] See Svennilson, op. cit., p. 259.

to most European countries. Nor must we overlook the fact that Sweden did not lose the flower of her youth. She escaped the tragedy of " the lost generation " : her human resources remained intact. How fortunate she was in this respect may be shown by a comparison of the age-distribution of her male population in 1921 with that of Great Britain, Germany, and France.

AGE DISTRIBUTION OF MALES BETWEEN THE AGES OF 15 AND 70.[1]

	Great Britain.		*Germany.*		*France.*		*Sweden.*	
	1911.	*1921.*	*1911.*	*1921.*	*1911.*	*1921.*	*1911.*	*1921.*
15–25 . .	133	123	146	137	115	112	140	140
25–35 . .	118	101	120	96	110	89	109	110
35–45 . .	98	95	95	93	98	93	83	90
45–55 . .	70	81	70	76	83	87	74	68
55–70 . .	60	70	61	63	84	89	77	79
	479	470	492	465	490	470	483	487

The War meant a terrible sacrifice of young life. The belligerent powers were soon able to repair their depleted capital resources; but the " lost generation " was irreplaceable. Sweden, however, emerged from the World Crisis with two important advantages: she had become a creditor instead of a debtor, and her population contained a normal proportion of youth.

[1] A. L. Bowley, op. cit., p. 55.

Chapter II

DIAGNOSIS AND REMEDIES

THE new problems caused by the War gave the economists plenty of food for thought; and we find Wicksell, Davidson, Cassel, and Heckscher endeavouring to diagnose the malady and offering advice to the practical men. The doctors were occasionally called in for consultation but for the most part they gave their opinions spontaneously. They seem to have been fairly unanimous as to the real nature of the disease, but they diverged in their interpretations of some of the queer symptoms. Their prescriptions, though based on sound economic physiology, were almost all rejected on the ground that the suggested cure was worse than the disease. In those rare cases when expert advice was accepted, the authorities took the precaution of administering a suitable antidote. The behaviour of those responsible for the patient was in the best traditions of rule of thumb medicine; and it is not surprising that in the most acute stage of the illness the experts were as much concerned about the dangerous effects of previous treatment as they were about the essential roots of the malady.

The survival of the patient was due chiefly to the fact that he had been blessed with a very strong constitution; and the presence of brilliant specialists was at least a guarantee that no fatal expedients would be tried. The fate of another sufferer—Germany—in 1923 illustrates what happens when both the practical men and the doctors are quite innocent of sound theoretical insight.

(1) Wicksell's Plan

We have already seen that one of the powerful causes of the inflation in Sweden was the very favourable demand for her exports and the liberal granting of foreign credits. Wicksell, Davidson, and Heckscher laid particular stress on this. Owing to the extreme scarcity of capital in the belligerent countries their "natural" rates were always in excess of that of Sweden. A banking policy which kept the money rate equal to the "natural" rate in Sweden (assuming that an approximation could be arrived at for practical purposes) would be of no avail to prevent a cumulative movement upwards, as long as Sweden maintained her trade relations with the rest of the world. Wicksell, recognizing the complicated character of the problem, made an ingenious proposal for putting the brake on the rise in prices.[1] In

[1] See "Medel mot dyrtiden," *E.T.*, 1916, p. 304.

brief he advocated a system of duties on exports and premiums on imports (or the sale by the State of imported goods below the import price). This would be sufficient to bring down the internal price level to the desired level, without having any effect on the exchange rate. Assuming the rate was at par, it could be maintained there, while the internal price level was pushed down.

The theory of the plan is as follows.[1] Assuming convertibility and free gold movements, we know that a rise in prices abroad will communicate itself to our country (*A*). If the Central Bank in *A* issues new notes the increase in prices will occur directly: otherwise there is a time lag during which exports exceed imports, gold flows in, and prices then rise to the new equilibrium level. We now postulate that *A* levies duties on exports and uses the proceeds to enable imported goods to be sold at a lower price on the home market. The result is a reversal of the process. Imports will tend to exceed exports, for, other things being equal, the whole volume of exports can only remain as profitable as before if the average price falls by the amount of the duty. There will be an outward movement of gold until the smaller reserve and the notes based on it are just sufficient to carry the goods transactions on the lower price level. This

[1] Ibid., p. 304 ff.

will constitute a new equilibrium. If the Bank in *A* had, according to our first assumption, issued new notes without an increase in its gold reserve, the reverse process would take place more quickly ; and it would be necessary to raise the discount rate to prevent an excessive outflow of gold. The exchange rate during the process would be unaffected. It would remain at par or merely move within the gold points.

Wicksell did not overlook the fact that the conditions of the time (namely, late 1916) diverged somewhat from the postulates of his proposal. He anticipated that, if the plan were put into operation then, the rate of exchange would move against Sweden and the krona-sterling exchange would soon be at par again. He would then advocate raising the discount rate to prevent it going further. For the purposes of the time Wicksell was accordingly inclined to combine two methods : on the one hand, relatively low export duties and, on the other, stiffer credit conditions in order to raise the gold value of the currency and exert a moderating influence on the price level.

Under this plan the relations between Swedish and foreign currencies would be quite independent of the relation between the price level in Sweden and price levels abroad. As against the criticism that foreigners, when they discovered that internal consumption was independent of the price of imports at the ports, would raise their prices drastically, Wicksell replied that competition in the world market would prevent such a development. Another possibility was that, if the internal demand proved elastic, the proceeds of the export duties might not suffice to defray the difference between the prices of imported goods at the ports and the prices at which they were sold on the home market. In that case Wicksell would be content with imperfect success. Davidson agreed that the plan was theoretically sound.

What Wicksell omitted to take into account was its possible effects on different groups of prices in Sweden. The practical problem of varying the rates of duty and premium, according as the conditions of supply of exports and imports changed, would also have to be faced.[1] But even ignoring this, it is hard to deny that such a two-fold interference would alter the relationships between the prices of goods in different stages of production. It might well be that, though the average internal price level might be lowered, the new margins between prices would be such as to stimulate further inflation. By analogy, we may refer to the effects of the Government's policy in keeping the prices of foodstuffs relatively low.

[1] See Davidson, " Om export afgifter och import premier såsom botemedel mot dyrtiden," *E.T.*, 1916, p. 347.

The Government and the Central Bank were not likely to accept this bold prescription. Even had they agreed with the reasoning and thought it practical to act upon it, they could never have swallowed a plan which was so "socialistic" in character. To this latter charge Wicksell could only reply innocently that he was merely endeavouring to check the forces which were radically altering the pre-War distribution of wealth.

(2) Discount Policy

On the role of the discount rate the economists were in fair agreement. Herr V. Moll, the Governor of the Riksbank, defended himself against their attacks [1] in an article in *Ekonomisk Tidskrift* in 1917.[2] He began by reminding his critics that it was only after the introduction of gold exclusion that the discount rate could have assumed any importance, and that the operation of that measure had been more or less nullified by the unavoidable imports of Scandinavian gold coin. In the opinion of the Governor there were two special circumstances which were influencing the value of the Swedish krona at the time, namely, the imports of securities and the granting of

[1] Particularly that of G. Cassel in *Dyrtiden och sedelöverflöd* (1917).

[2] V. Moll, "Riksbanken och dyrtiden," *E.T.*, 1917, No. 7, p. 69.

credit to foreign countries. These two factors were traceable to the natural desire of foreigners to settle their obligations to Sweden on the most favourable terms. Herr Moll asserted that, as the Riksbank had no control over these forces, it could not be held responsible for their effects. Furthermore, the influence of a rise in the bank rate by one or two points had become negligible. The prospects of profit were so rosy that the entrepreneurs were not frightened by movements in their interest charges. If the rate were put up to an extremely high level, the effect on businesses which were not taking part in the feverish speculative boom would be disastrous. Such was the gist of the Governor's self-defence. He concluded his article in the following words : "The Riksbank has during the War sought to maintain contact with our economists and they have very readily placed their opinion, reports, and advice at its disposal. The economists' view that the Bank should pay more attention to their advice than it does, is easy to understand. But the Bank has to take all sorts of circumstances into account. . . . When Cassel declares that the fault is wholly that of the Bank and that the popular idea that profiteers influence prices is false, the layman merely turns away, reflecting what a curious science economics is." [1]

The actual discount policy pursued by the

[1] Loc. cit., p. 279.

Riksbank was often open to criticism. There were occasions when conditions clearly demanded a raising of the loan rate, whereas the Bank actually lowered it. Such was the situation immediately after the inauguration of the gold exclusion policy, when on the 1st May, 1916, the rate was reduced from $5\frac{1}{2}$ to 5 per cent.[1]

The lack of confidence of the authorities in the efficiency of this instrument is shown by the fact that in 1917, the year of intense speculation and rising prices, the rate did not reach 6 per cent until September. The recession which came after the Armistice was misinterpreted by the Riksbank and the rate was reduced from 7 per cent to $6\frac{1}{2}$ in April, 1919, and again to 6 per cent in June. This policy could not but aggravate the intensity of the boom which was to reach its peak in the following year.

(3) The Rationing of Credit

The circumstances of the War made it inevitable that a part of Sweden's capital should be commandeered by other countries. Irrespective of the height of the rate of interest in Sweden the process would have gone on. Cassel argued that " it would have been far

[1] At that time the imports of gold coin from Norway and Denmark had not begun to vitiate gold exclusion.

better if Sweden had continued to allow gold free access as under normal conditions and had thus allowed the purchasing power of its currency to be regulated by that of gold. Its whole circulation might have been covered by gold ; and the loss of interest would have been insignificant compared with what the Bank had to write off afterwards on its foreign assets ".[1] It is not obvious that this would have necessarily been to the greater advantage of the country. There were two courses open to Sweden. If she had maintained a very high discount rate in order to protect the value of the currency, the discrepancy between the Swedish and the world price level would have induced a gold inflow which would have led to a rise of internal prices. In this case Sweden would have been compelled to receive gold against the export of capital and the volume of credits granted to foreign countries would have been smaller. On the other hand, if the country had kept a relatively low discount rate, the increase in the note circulation would have kept pace with that of other countries and there would have been no incentive for a gold influx. In this case Sweden's capital would have been placed at the disposal of foreigners mainly in the form of credits. It is important to notice that in either case a substantial export of capital was bound to take

[1] *Money and Foreign Exchange after 1914*, p. 94.

place.[1] If gold exclusion was to achieve its object, it should at least have been accompanied by a discount rate well above the level which was "normal" to current internal Swedish conditions.

The failure of this policy in practice to stop the deterioration in the internal value of the currency led Davidson to suggest practical measures of curtailing foreign lending. Capital was so scarce in the belligerent countries that there was an appreciable margin between the "natural" rate in those countries and in Sweden. Obstacles were being placed in the way of imports, but the demand for exports was insatiable. Swedish capitalists, unlike their English prototypes referred to by Ricardo, lacked the sense of patriotism which would prompt them to invest at home though the rate of interest (with an allowance for risk) abroad was higher. Davidson, therefore, drew up a memorandum outlining a concrete plan for cutting down the volume of foreign credits; but it was never published.[2]

In June, 1918, the Minister of Finance appointed a Committee to inquire into the monetary situation. It consisted of three professional economists (Professors Davidson, Wicksell, and Brisman) and three bank

[1] See Davidson, "Riksbankens sedelutgifning," *E.T.*, 1918, p. 96 ff.

[2] See Heckscher in *Sweden, Norway, Denmark, and Iceland in the World War*, p. 210.

directors, under the chairmanship of the Governor of the Riksbank. The economists and the bankers naturally disagreed about most things [1]; but they managed to reach a unanimous decision on one matter. It was proposed that there should be a " qualitative rationing of capital requirements " together with a stricter regulation of foreign lending. The proposal was severely criticized by Professor Heckscher [2] who was of the view that the only way to damp down the optimistic anticipations of the business world was to raise the discount rate boldly to the necessary level. Davidson took a more practical view of the situation and defended the project by emphasizing the serious depletion of Sweden's capital resources owing to abnormal foreign lending and the absence of borrowing.[3] He was not prepared merely to rely on a high discount rate, though he did not want the rate to be lowered during the experiment of rationing. As a result of the inquiry a Capital Control Board, under the auspices of the Central Bank, was actually formed in October, 1918; it was to supervise the flotation of new companies, capital issues, and bond issues of a minimum of 100,000 kronor. It was a very

[1] See *Betänkande rörande åtgärder för penningvärdets reglering* (Official Publications, 1918).

[2] See " Frågan om penningens reglering," *E.T.*, 1918.

[3] See " Ransonering av kapital," *E.T.*, 1918, No. 8, p. 267 ff., and " Ransonering av kapital än en gång," *E.T.*, 1918, p. 289 ff.

modest version of the Committee's proposals; but it did not come to fruition as the Armistice completely altered the situation.

The problem with which the Banking Committee had to grapple was by no means simple. The attitude of the critics who merely denounced the authorities for not raising the bank rate high enough was neither fully justified nor helpful. The "rate of interest" which is of importance for investment is not one single rate; there are several rates. Furthermore, any one of them does not in itself measure the price of capital to the entrepreneur, for the credit may be granted on various conditions of which the rate is only one. The cost to the borrower is, therefore, the net result of a combination of conditions which the Bank imposes. If the bank rate was to be a deterrent during the War boom it would have had to be raised to 12 or 14 per cent. But, used in this way, it would have been a double-edged weapon. Enterprise in agriculture, quarrying, building, and house property would have been gravely injured. The real problem was whether there was an alternative to this indiscriminate punishment of the just as well as the unjust. There is strong reason for thinking that, not only in an abnormal war-time boom but in any upward swing, due recognition of the heterogeneity of interest rates and the need for differentiation would greatly enhance the moderating influence of bank policy.

The possibilities of effective discrimination are normally very limited; and in the case of bank credit it is almost impossible to hit upon a satisfactory criterion.[1] There are, broadly speaking, short-term and long-term loans; or credits may be graded according to the type of security on which they rest; or again according to the length of life of the investment in which they are tied up. A distinction might be made between export and domestic credits; or between the replacement of old capital and "new investment". Finally one could differentiate capital demands according to their elasticity. Any attempt at discrimination by the banks would give an incentive to certain borrowers to take credit at the relatively lower rate and then undercut the bank by relending. It would doubtless have been possible to load the dice against export credits in Sweden during the War; and there is evidence that the Riksbank was very half-hearted in the pursuit of this end. The practical difficulties of discrimination according to the uses of capital are very considerable. Professor Lindahl is, however, of the opinion that, if it were practically feasible, the banks would be performing a valuable service by treating loans for new

[1] See E. Lindahl, *Penningpolitikens medel* (1930), pp. 51–68, for a very useful discussion of this subject.

capital investments differently from credits for replacement.[1] The former are obviously much more sensitive to changes in the interest rate.

A full analysis of this problem would lead us to consider the significance of the demand for credit exercised by the State and public bodies. It has been suggested elsewhere that this demand can ordinarily be classified as relatively inelastic.[2] Where public and semi-public enterprise is an important factor in the capital market and corporate saving by private companies has assumed large proportions, the case for discrimination in the fixing of credit conditions becomes stronger. The Swedish Banking Committee's proposals were on the right lines but the implications of rationing and discrimination were not adequately realized.

(4) The Exchange Rate and the Price Level

It remains to seek an explanation for the coincidence of a premium on Swedish currency in terms of the dollar and sterling with a considerable rise in the Swedish price level relatively to that of the United States and Great Britain. The facts are set out in the following table,[3] and are illustrated in the diagram.

Professor Davidson, in his analysis of war-

[1] Op. cit., p. 62.
[2] See *Unbalanced Budgets*, part ii, Germany, p. 205.
[3] See Davidson, "Riksbanken och penningens värde under kristiden," *E.T.*, 1925, p. 13.

time inflation, always laid stress on the part played by physical scarcity of commodities. It is very difficult to weight this particular factor; but he was not prepared to share Cassel's view

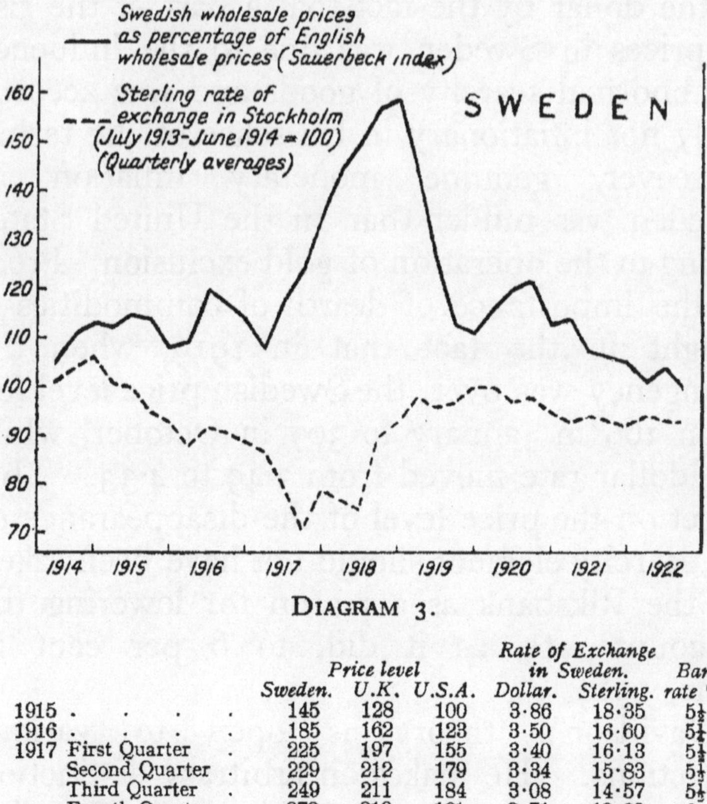

DIAGRAM 3.

	Price level			Rate of Exchange in Sweden.		Bank
	Sweden.	*U.K.*	*U.S.A.*	*Dollar.*	*Sterling.*	*rate %.*
1915	145	128	100	3·86	18·35	5½
1916	185	162	123	3·50	16·60	5½
1917 First Quarter .	225	197	155	3·40	16·13	5½
Second Quarter .	229	212	179	3·34	15·83	5½
Third Quarter .	249	211	184	3·08	14·57	5½
Fourth Quarter .	272	219	181	2·71	12·83	6
1918 January . .	299	223	185	3·03	14·22	7
April . . .	322	227	191	2·99	14·09	7
July . .	333	231	198	2·82	13·41	7
October . .	370	237	204	3·39	16·08	7

that it was of minor importance. According to Davidson's theory the situation in the period from the beginning of 1917 to the autumn of 1918 was dominated by four factors, namely, the special prohibitions which the belligerents placed on Swedish imports, the gold exclusion policy, the nature of the internal inflation, and speculation in foreign exchange. He explained the appreciation of the Swedish krona in terms of the dollar by the fact that a part of the rise in prices in Sweden was due to the influence of abnormal scarcity of goods and was accordingly not inflationary in his sense of the term; moreover, genuine monetary inflation in Sweden was milder than in the United States owing to the operation of gold exclusion. Proof of the importance of dearth of commodities is sought in the fact that in 1919, when the stringency was over, the Swedish price level fell from 369 in January to 307 in October, while the dollar rate moved from 3·49 to 4·35. This effect on the price level of the disappearance of the scarcity element should not have been taken by the Riksbank as a reason for lowering the discount rate, as it did, to 6 per cent in June, 1919.

Davidson's theory is open to various objections. He makes an arbitrary distinction between two elements in the rise in the Swedish price level, namely, physical scarcity and genuine monetary inflation. He makes an allowance for the former and appears to think that it is only the rise in prices which would have taken place without it which is relevant to the connection between relative price levels and the exchange rate. It may be conceded that for certain purposes monetary theory has to distinguish between a rise in prices due to scarcity of goods and that which is the effect of an increase in the quantity of money. But, given certain assumptions regarding domestic and international goods, a rise in the price level relatively to other countries may be expected to have a parallel influence on the rate of exchange, irrespective of the causes which have led to the rise in prices. Davidson regarded a rise in the price level due to physical scarcity as a " change in the value of goods " and not a " change in the value of money "; and from this he jumped to the conclusion that this part of the rise in the price level would not influence the exchange rates in the same way as monetary inflation. No valid reason can be advanced for this proposition.[1]

War-time circumstances were, however, abnormal. Let us examine, first, the situation which arose between the United States and the European belligerents. There was an enormous demand for American products, and freight rates for the eastward voyage across the Atlantic reached fantastic heights. For this reason alone the average price level on this side was bound to be higher than in the United States. The sterling-dollar rate of exchange remained at par. What is the explanation ? Faced with an

[1] For further comments on Professor Davidson's theory of money, see my article " The Monetary Doctrines of Professor Davidson," *Economic Journal*, March, 1935, pp. 36–50.

import surplus England could do one of two things. She could raise her rate of interest to the point where it would be worth while for the American creditors to postpone the realization of their claims; or she could prohibit gold exports and thus allow the rate of exchange to move against her. What actually happened was that England pegged the exchange rate and sold British-owned American securities or pledged them in the United States. This was tantamount to raising the rate of interest, for the quotations had to be driven low enough to tempt the Americans to accept the bargain. The sterling-dollar rate could be kept at par only by guaranteeing the American creditors a much higher interest rate than would otherwise have prevailed.[1]

If England had merely put a formal ban on the export of gold (the ban was, of course, effective in practice), then sterling would have depreciated in terms of the dollar. The rate of exchange, which would be the outcome of this process, would not be decided by the relation between the price levels but by the *anticipations* of English debtors and American creditors regarding the future value of the currencies. As Wicksell has pointed out, exchange speculation would play a fundamental part. The higher the premium on the dollar,

[1] See K. Wicksell, "Växelkursernas gåta," *E.T.*, 1919, for a valuable discussion of the subject.

the more likely the Americans would be to purchase English securities with the intention of selling at a higher price later. At the same time Englishmen would have an incentive to sell American securities in the hope of repurchasing in the future at a lower price in sterling. When the rate of exchange reached the level where these acts of speculation could take place, it would not move any farther away from parity.

The problem of the sterling-krona rate of exchange during the War can only be interpreted logically in the light of this reasoning. England had an adverse balance with Sweden; but she did not peg the exchange and counterbalance it by giving the creditors a sufficiently high rate of interest on postponed claims. She allowed sterling to depreciate in terms of the krona and the limit to this depreciation depended largely on the anticipations of the Swedish creditors regarding the future value of sterling. When the War was going badly for the Allies, the anticipated exchange profit needed to satisfy the Swedes would naturally have to be rather high. As the War drew to a close the anticipations would be revised and the rate would tend to move towards parity.

There were special factors which helped to explain why the Swedish price level rose more than that of England and U.S.A. The enormous freight rates on imported goods, the prohibitions which seriously curtailed the volume of imports, the conditions of demand for exports, and internal monetary and financial policy worked in this direction. The important fact to notice, however, is that, given a large export surplus and a policy of gold exclusion, the krona rate in terms of the currencies of debtor countries was bound to appreciate to the point where the possibility of a future exchange profit was sufficiently attractive to compensate the creditors for postponing the realization of their claims. It is not surprising that the problem of curtailing foreign credits was so difficult.

War-time inflation in a neutral country is a complicated phenomenon of extraordinary interest. As long as the external situation was allowed to exercise unrestricted influence on the course of internal prices and production, it was impossible to avoid an extreme inflation. The maxim of the " normal " rate of interest, i.e. the maintenance of a bank rate equal to the " natural " rate—one of the most important fruits of pre-war Swedish economics—was of very little use. In any case the reasoning lying behind this precept is based on the assumption of a closed system. Production in Sweden during the War was increasingly under the domination of the enormous demand of foreign countries for Swedish raw materials and capital goods. Even if there were such a thing as "*the* natural rate" which could have been approximately measured, it would not have been an adequate guide for banking policy.

We must conclude that drastic interference along the lines of Wicksell's plan would have been necessary, if the flood of internal inflation was to be stemmed. Gold exclusion should have been supplemented by State control of imports and exports. The proceeds of stiff duties on exports should have been used to lower the prices of imported goods on the home market. The lower internal price level would have eased the budgetary problem; and, as we have shown, factors of production would have moved into domestic industries such as agriculture. The whole experiment would have left the exchange rate more or less undisturbed. The boom might also have been checked if wages, in the early stage, had not lagged so far behind the prices of industrial products. Under these new conditions production would be directed more towards satisfying the home market, and the volume of foreign credits would automatically be curtailed. There would still be the possibility, however, that the plan would distort price margins within Sweden in such a way as to generate further inflation; but this would have been of a smaller order of magnitude and of a character different from the cumulative process which actually took place. Once the fantastic expectations of profits in the export trade had been damped down, the capital goods industries would be influenced more by the course of domestic prices. Discount policy would again come into its own. It was admittedly a choice between evils ; but, assuming it could have been translated into practice, such a plan as this would have certainly been the lesser evil.

(5) Capital Exports and " Forced Savings "

It is clear from the foregoing analysis that the problem of an open system has special features. When a small country has a relatively large export trade in instrumental goods, it must be regarded as a part of a " structure of production ", the lowest stage of which is located in other countries. The economic system can thus be divided into two sections. One consists of the export trades together with the constructional and machine-making industries ranged behind them ; the other comprises the industries producing for the home market, their final output being chiefly consumers' goods. The domestic " structure " exercises a demand for some of the capital goods produced in the exporting group. The income disbursed in both sections is allocated partly to home consumption goods, partly to foreign consumption goods, and partly to saving. The savings are used to replace capital in the domestic and the export groups, to extend equipment in one or the other or in both, and for foreign investment, short-term and long-term.

Assuming a gold standard and an export of capital from such a country owing to a discrepancy between interest rates, part of the domestic savings will be invested abroad. If this means that certain replacements will not be made at home, it will have a serious effect on the values of the capital goods concerned. The tendency will be towards contraction in the home country and expansion in the importing country.[1]

In the case of Sweden during the War the course of events was quite different. The following phenomena were found together: continuous capital exports, a rapid rise in the price-level, a fall in physical productivity, an expansion in the note circulation which, when the boom was in full swing, was faster than the rise in prices.

It is an interesting example of a species of "forced saving" in an open system, due to a change in circumstances abroad. The export of capital took several forms. Swedish exporters accumulated claims on their foreign debtors. They either kept them as assets or handed them to the banks in exchange for Swedish currency. Foreign securities were purchased

[1] Cf. R. Nurkse, *Internationale Kapitalbewegungen* (1935), pp. 194–9.

by Swedish nationals ; and, as we have shown, the low quotations at which these transactions would be made were equivalent to a high rate of interest on the capital sent abroad. The banks themselves would also grant credits to foreign countries where the exported products were marketed. In this way purchasing power was prepared beforehand for the output of Swedish industries. Savings which would otherwise have been necessary for replacement purposes at home, to say nothing of extensions of equipment, were thus being regularly transferred abroad. This loss of capital, far from leading to contraction in the exporting country, actually proved a powerful stimulus. The unbounded prosperity in the export industries sent capital values soaring ; expectations became extremely optimistic ; and resources moved from the domestic to the export section. Hence an enormous demand for credit, to which the elastic currency system responded automatically. The following figures [1] show the relative rate of increase in wholesale prices and the note circulation in Sweden during the War.

Percentage Increase in the last Quarter of the Year over the Corresponding Period in the Previous Year

	1915	1916	1917	1918
Wholesale Prices	29·2	34·8	30·2	36·0
Note Circulation	7·1	24·4	39·3	47·0

In the early phase of the boom prices rose faster than the note circulation. But there

[1] E. Heckscher, *Penningväsende och penningpolitik*, op. cit., p. 85.

was a substantial rise in the velocity of circulation, due to the rapid development of the cheque system. It is estimated that from the outbreak of the War to the end of 1915 there was an increase of 65·5 per cent in current accounts compared with only 6·7 per cent in bank deposits as a whole.[1] Moreover, in the first two years of the War, there was some uncertainty about the continuance of prosperity in the export trade. In 1917 and 1918 the expansion in the volume of money far outran the rise in prices. The savings transferred abroad were offset by a much larger volume of "forced savings". The rise in the price level was intensified by the artificial restriction on imports and the fall in the physical productivity of labour.

It is important to realize that a comparison between the "money rate" and the "natural rate" loses all meaning in these circumstances. Nor is it legitimate to compare the "natural rate" in Sweden and in the capital importing countries. The two were not independent. As profits rose in the belligerent countries, so would the expected rate of return increase in the Swedish export trades. The two "natural rates" would therefore move together; and the transference of capital from Sweden had no tendency to diminish the disparity, but, on the contrary, generated further forced saving and inflation in the exporting country.

[1] Ibid., p. 48.

CHAPTER III

SWEDISH MONETARY THEORY SINCE WICKSELL

(1) THE LEGACY OF WICKSELL AND DAVIDSON

MODERN monetary theory in Sweden is founded mainly on the work of Wicksell and Davidson. Wicksell's famous doctrine of the normal rate of interest, which has left a deep mark on subsequent analysis, was not taken at its face value by his fellow economists. Criticisms which have received general recognition in other countries in the last decade were a commonplace in Sweden before the War. The credit for this is chiefly due to Professor Davidson.[1]

The argument in Wicksell's *Geldzins und Güterpreise* was that the value of money would remain constant, i.e. the general level of prices would be stable, as long as the loan rate of interest was normal, i.e. equal to the " natural " rate. As early as 1906 Davidson had pointed out a serious weakness in this doctrine ; and the essence of his objection may be gleaned from the following quotation. " All changes

[1] See my article on " The Monetary Doctrines of Professor Davidson ", *Economic Journal*, March, 1935, pp. 36–50.

in the general level of prices do not constitute changes in the value of money. When productivity increases, the requirement that the value of money should remain stable demands that prices should fall: when the production of goods increases without a rise in productivity, the same requirement demands that the price level should remain stable. . . . An increase in production may be the reflection both of the growth of population and capital and of a rise in productivity; and the necessity of keeping these two sets of factors apart makes the task of monetary management very difficult. The problem is not so simple as Wicksell seems to think." [1]

When Wicksell came to write his *Lectures on Political Economy* he had changed his position to some extent. In *Geldzins und Güterpreise* he held the view that every movement of the general price level is to be attributed to a discrepancy between the money and the natural rate. In the *Lectures*, however, he conceded that an increase in the supply of gold or an issue of paper money can lead to a rise in the price level even though the loan rate of interest is "normal". But he never admitted that Davidson's main criticism was justified, though there are sentences in the last article he wrote which suggest that at the end of his life he was

[1] "Något om begreppet penningens värde," *E.T.*, 1906, pp. 457–8.

prepared for a drastic revision of his doctrine.[1] It is often remarked that the abnormal inflationary experience of the War and post-War periods threw a vivid light on old academic truths; but it also taught the economist that there are still many things which need explanation.

In view of the use which has been made of Wicksell's concepts in modern trade cycle theory, it is pertinent to inquire whether Wicksell and Davidson were thinking of cyclical fluctuations in their controversies regarding the normal rate of interest. The evidence indicates that they were not. In the last chapter of *Geldzins und Güterpreise*, where Wicksell attempts to relate his theory to reality, the price movements examined are of the secular kind, e.g. 1851–1873 and 1873–1896. Some economists, e.g. Johan Åkerman, are of the opinion that the Wicksellian construction should be read in this light.[2] The second volume of the *Lectures* contains a special note on "The Business Cycle and Crises" which says that the underlying cause of fluctuations is to be found in the irregularity of technical advance. The exploitation of each wave of invention means an enormous transformation of free

[1] K. Wicksell, "Das Valutaproblem in den skandinavischen Ländern," originally published in Swedish in *E.T.*, 1925, No. 10–11.

[2] See J. Åkerman, *Om det ekonomiska livets rytmik* (1928), pp. 266–7.

capital into fixed long-lasting investment which starts the upward swing. Furthermore, in a polemic against another Swedish economist, Professor Brock, in *Ekonomisk Tidskrift* in 1909, Wicksell wrote, " I have never sought to explain *konjunktur* changes, i.e. boom and slump, on the basis of a deviation of the money rate from the natural rate. Their real cause lies in the irregularity of technical progress and the influence of psychological elements. I believe that the reaction from boom to slump, i.e. the crisis in the narrow sense, has its roots in the monetary sphere, in a faulty money and bank policy." [1] We shall see in later chapters that the emphasis on individuals' anticipations is a marked feature of recent Swedish theory. The fact, however, that the author of the apparatus of the natural rate did not apply it to the trade cycle problem does not mean that it is incapable of providing part of the solution of that problem.

With the death of Wicksell in 1925 it may be said that an epoch in Swedish economic thought came to an end. His propositions regarding the money and the natural rate had brought monetary theory into organic connection with general equilibrium theory. He did this by asking what happens if the rate of interest, or the price ratio between present and future goods, in terms of money, deviates

[1] *E.T.*, 1909, p. 61.

from the natural rate of equilibrium theory. It was only a short step from this formulation of the problem to the Savings-Investment analysis which is so typical of recent monetary theory. The creative work of the master was supplemented by the acute criticism of Davidson. It was he who first demonstrated that, to use the words of Professor Robbins, " the proposition that the money rate of interest which keeps the price level stable is also the rate which clears the market of voluntarily accumulated capital, breaks down when the conditions of capital supply are either progressive or retrogressive." [1] The ground was thus cleared for a new attack on the theory of fluctuation. The young generation of Swedish economists were fortunate in their rich legacy. It was a significant portent that in 1927 there appeared from the pen of Professor Gunnar Myrdal a book on Risk and Equilibrium Theory [2] which proved to be the opening of a new epoch in Swedish economics.

(2) Economic Dynamics

In building up an explanation of the determination of prices the economist makes three broad approximations. First he sets out the conditions of static equilibrium: the basic

[1] Introduction to Wicksell's *Lectures on Political Economy*, vol. i (1934), p. xvii.
[2] *Prisbildningsproblemet och föränderligheten* (1927).

assumption is that individuals act on the knowledge that there will be no future changes of data. The second case, which may be called quasi-static, covers the situation where future changes are accurately foreseen and people dispose of their resources in the light of this perfect foresight. The economist comes nearest to reality in the third stage when he takes into account the fact that the future is only imperfectly foreseen, and that resources are invested under the shadow of uncertainty.

The theory of static equilibrium now commands general assent. The economist feels that here he has firm ground under his feet. He is able to seize upon essentials and give a satisfactory explanation of some of the fundamental forces at work in the real world. But when he faces the problem of cyclical fluctuation he cannot help feeling that the assumptions of accurate foresight and perfect adjustment are grave handicaps. He has excluded the all-important factor of risk. It is a commonplace that production takes time, and it means binding together free resources in a more or less fixed form. During the life-time of an investment changes take place either in technical conditions or in the value of the product. Economic risk is due chiefly to the fact of immobility. Changes in the relevant data are never perfectly foreseen, nor do they usually occur as complete surprises. Individuals view them as degrees of probability. The investor is confronted with various prospects to which he may attach quantitative value. We must distinguish between his estimate of the objective probability, the degree of faith he has in his own judgment,[1] and his gambling preference. The boundary lines between the more risky and the less risky investments are continually shifting; and alterations in people's subjective attitudes to their risks can have a profound effect on the total volume of investment.

The textbooks often refer to "normal" prices around which the prices of the real world are supposed to fluctuate. But the standard with which actual prices are to be compared is not that based on such static assumptions. It is necessary to inquire into the influence exerted on exchange and production by the fact that the future is imperfectly foreseen. This is the problem of Economic Dynamics. In his book on Equilibrium Theory and Change, Professor Myrdal has shown that static theory has to be developed in at least two directions.[2] There is, first, the bearing of uncertainty on the prices of final goods and of factors of production and, secondly, its influence on the proportions in which entrepreneurs combine their resources.

[1] Cf. F. H. Knight, *Risk, Uncertainty, and Profit* (1921), p. 225.
Prisbildningsproblemet och föränderligheten, chapter i.

The latter means nothing less than a completely revised theory of production. When a producer purchases free resources and invests them in the form of fixed plant, he knows that they cannot be released and adapted to new circumstances except at a certain cost. If he is wise, he will try to estimate the probable trend of technical invention in the industry and the influences likely to affect future costs and the value of the product. Professor Myrdal, in his analysis of the theory of production, enumerates three decisions involved in the act of investment.[1] The producer has to determine, first, the scale of output, secondly, how durable his fixed plant is to be, and, lastly, the proportion which prime costs (wages, raw materials, fuel, etc.) shall bear to fixed capital charges (interest, amortization, etc.). The amount of capital sunk in the investment depends on these three factors. Static theory assumes that present and future prices are known and are not affected by the particular combination adopted by the entrepreneur. The problem is then handled by assuming any two of the factors as given and varying the other; and it can be shown how the best combination is achieved.

To be realistic, however, we have to recognize that, when the entrepreneur is determining his best combination, he is facing an uncertain

[1] Op. cit., chapter xi.

future.[1] He makes shrewd guesses as to probable changes in technique and in costs and prices. His estimate of risks and his degree of faith in his own foresight will, for example, influence his decision concerning the scale of output. The larger the undertaking, the greater is the opportunity open to the entrepreneur to insure against certain risks. There will be a point at which the diseconomies of a larger output will exactly offset the advantages of being in a better position to reduce uncertainty. Moreover, his decision on the durability of his plant will be affected by his views regarding the price of his product during future periods of time. There will be an incentive to choose less durable machinery, if he rates the risk highly in later periods.

Professor Myrdal has endeavoured to give the risk element its proper place within the framework of pure theory. If one regards immobility as a friction which can be safely ignored, one is ruling out the fact which has most to do with risk. Lack of mobility means a plus for costs and either a plus or a minus for incomes, and it must, therefore, be included with the other elements determining prices.

(3) Profits and Losses

The theory of profit is associated with uncertainty ; and Professor Myrdal has done

[1] Op. cit., chapter xiii.

much to clarify the connection. The notion of capital value rests upon anticipations of an imperfectly foreseen future. Let us enumerate the elements which make up the value of a capital instrument. The owner calculates (*a*) the receipts he expects to obtain during the life-time of the investment, (*b*) the costs during the same period, and (*c*) the rate of interest likely to prevail in the future. These are intelligent guesses ; the investor may feel quite confident that they are near the mark but, on the other hand, he may be conscious of a wide margin of error. This valuation of risk must be included in the computation of capital value. The receipts and costs, corrected by reference to the degree of risk, are capitalized according to the expected future rate of interest. The difference between these two sums represents the present value of the capital.

When the investment is made, its value is governed by the owner's expectations at that moment. If, in a year's time, the demand for his product has fallen and his receipts are below what he anticipated, he will then change his views about the future. The difference between the income he now expects and his original estimate constitutes a " loss " ; and, assuming that nothing else has changed, the capital value of his investment will fall by the amount of the loss. Thus, when anything happens which alters the basis of capitalizing future incomes and costs, even if it be a weakening or a strengthening of the owner's confidence in his estimates, a net " profit " or a " loss " occurs and the value of the capital will rise or fall correspondingly. Profits and losses are, therefore, not prices but adjustments in capital value.[1]

Some economists of the Austrian School have made great play of the bogy of " capital consumption ". We have been told that the extensive building of working-class flats by the Social Democrats in Vienna after the War was a gross example of the wasting of a poor country's substance. Other countries have been warned against this insidious disease. The theory upon which these deductions are based is not very convincing. No satisfactory explanation is given of what is meant by keeping capital intact.[2] If we employ the concepts of the Swedish economists, we can at least arrive at a logical definition of " capital consumption "; but it cannot be used to support easy generalizations about policy. Suppose cotton planters obtain a larger crop than they expected and they can sell the whole of it at the anticipated price. They receive a " profit " equal to the excess of their actual receipts over what they expected. In other words, the value of their capital has risen. But if the planters use all their profit for

[1] Myrdal, op cit., pp. 43–4.

[2] This is admitted by Dr. Hayek in his article " The Maintenance of Capital," *Economica*, 1935.

the purchase of consumption goods, they are eating up part of their capital.[1]

Professor Lindahl has shown that, if the concept of income is used in this way, saving can be logically defined as a part of income. Income is regarded as interest in the widest sense, namely, the continuous appreciation of capital goods due to the passage of time. Capital value rises as the discounted services come nearer and nearer: as the services are consumed capital value is reduced. "During a unit period this fall in value due to consumption may be greater or less than the appreciation due to the passage of time. The difference between interest and consumption equals Saving." [2]

The most interesting problems for the economist are presented by price risks, rather than unexpected changes in technique. Professor Knight distinguishes between "statistical probabilities" and rough "estimates". The former are based on a study of a large group of cases; but "the ordinary decisions of life are made on the basis of 'estimates' of a crude and superficial character".[3] This distinction is not very helpful. Price risks are characterized by the fact of moral hazard and the fact that

[1] Strictly speaking, there is no inroad into capital so long as the sum devoted to consumption is not greater than the interest on the addition to their capital value. See E. Lindahl, *Penningpolitikens medel*, p. 24.

[2] E. Lindahl, "The Concept of Income," *Essays in Honour of Cassel*.

[3] F. H. Knight, *Risk, Uncertainty, and Profit*, p. 210.

the law of large numbers is not applicable owing to biased movements.[1] It is on this account that the principle of insurance has its limits: measurability is not important.

An attempt has been made here to indicate one or two problems raised by Economic Dynamics.[2] It is this kind of analysis that is most likely to throw light on the causes of industrial fluctuations. In the words of Professor Myrdal, "a theory of prices, into which the factor of anticipations has been worked, is the most that analytical economics can do in interpreting a dynamic world."[3] The Swedish economists have recognized this fact; and for them the trade cycle is one problem in the general field of Economic Dynamics. It is no accident that the theory of fluctuation has been best handled by those economists who are aware of the significance of risk. Professor Pigou, in his important book on Industrial Fluctuations, emphasized the psychological elements in the problem. Those who criticized him for abandoning purely economic argument and resorting to a psycho-

[1] *Prisbildningsproblemet . . .*, pp. 109, 167.

[2] Important contributions have been made by Dr. J. R. Hicks in "Gleichgewicht und Konjunktur", *Zeitschrift für Nationalökonomie* 1933, and "Wages and Interest: the Dynamic Problem", *The Economic Journal*, 1935, and by Dr. P. Rosenstein-Rodan in "The Role of Time in Economic Theory", *Economica*, February, 1934. Mr. J. M. Keynes's new work, *The General Theory of Employment, Interest, and Money* (1936), will have a profound influence on future work in this field.

[3] Op. cit., p. 21.

logical explanation failed to appreciate the essential point of the book. One may have a verbal objection to the phrase "psychological theory"; but one cannot possibly get away from the fact that entrepreneurs' anticipations of future changes lie at the core of the problem of fluctuations. Failure to realize this has seriously handicapped those economists who start from the theory of the roundabout process of production. Dr. J. R. Hicks put his finger on a fundamental truth when he pointed out that "the whole problem of applying monetary theory is largely one of deducing changes in anticipations from the changes in objective data which call them forth".[1]

[1] "A Suggestion for Simplifying the Theory of Money," *Economica*, February, 1935, p. 13.

In his book *The Problem of Credit Policy* (1935), Mr. E. F. M. Durbin includes the factor of immobility in his monetary analysis; but his method is open to criticism because he does not specify his assumptions regarding foresight. He argues that "the result of an injection of new money into the structure of production depends on (*a*) the position and duration of the injection; (*b*) the type of price and distributional change brought about (influenced by the rigidity of money contracts, etc.); and (*c*) the relative speeds of adjustment of monetary quantities and physical quantities". To explain the effect of relative immobility on the process of adjustment Mr. Durbin makes use of two conceptions—"the average period of mobility" and "the average period of transaction velocity". "The period of mobility is the period of time within which the representative unit of labour or land can be and will be transferred to another position in the structure of production in which its money reward is greater than in its previous position—allowing for cost of transfer." The average period of transaction velocity is defined as "the number of times the representative unit of money exchanges against goods or property rights of any kind in the unit period". Let us imagine the familiar diagram of the successive stages in the structure of production. We assume that a certain quantity of money is injected in stage A. As the new money is diffused through the

(4) Means and Ends in Monetary Policy

The legacy of Wicksell and Davidson together with Myrdal's pioneering work on risk had paved the way for a new departure in the theory of monetary policy. The promise was amply fulfilled in Professor Erik Lindahl's studies on " Monetary Policy : the End and the Means ".[1] At the very outset the author strikes a new and significant note. A rational monetary policy is one which best realizes the end one

structure, it creates price differences between the stages. Mr. Durbin's argument then runs as follows : " If the period of mobility is equal to the period of transaction velocity then in period 2 there will be a rapid flow of resources to stage A. But by the time they have reached this position the whole situation has changed for now stage B is the profitable stage for primary factors. The previous flow to stage A will be reversed and a new flow to stage B will begin. But this is already too late since the profitable stages in period 4 have become stages C and Z. The resultant confusion and wastage of resources is obvious." (See pages 43–57.)

The definition of the " period of mobility " allows for cost of transfer. The cost of moving a factor must be conceived to be a sum per unit of time spread over the period during which its owner anticipates that he will be able to employ it profitably in the new position. Given the total cost, the sum per unit of time will clearly be greater, the shorter the period during which the entrepreneur expects the new position to be remunerative. Mr. Durbin, in the passage quoted above, tacitly assumes that the entrepreneur is ignorant of the probable effect of transaction velocity on future differences between prices in various stages of production. His argument is very unreal because he does not make clear what he is assuming about people's foresight. The costs of movement will vary with the entrepreneur's anticipations of (*a*) the period during which his resources will yield a profit in the new position ; (*b*) the loss of earnings during the transference and (*c*) his estimate of the margin of error.

Mr. Durbin's conclusions regarding policy have several points of affinity with those of Swedish theorists.

[1] *Penningpolitikens mål och medel* (1930).

regards as desirable; and the general end proposed is the diminution of economic risks and the friction which they create. One commendable thing about modern Swedish economists is that they are careful to be explicit when they assume a particular end to be desirable. The goal which Lindahl suggests is, of course, disputable. Everyone does not agree that it is desirable to diminish risks and economic friction. The business of the economist, however, is to take a given end, define it in concrete terms, and then consider the various ways in which it may be achieved.

Lindahl sums up his analysis under three heads. First, he has to decide the criterion by which the price level of consumption goods is to be regulated, (*a*) in a country on an independent paper standard, (*b*) in countries having an international standard in common. Secondly, is a free standard in each country preferable to an international standard? Thirdly, what means should be used to control the price level in different cases? The first question resolves itself into a choice between a stable price level of consumption goods and a price level varying inversely with productivity. The latter objective is chosen on the ground that it would be more effective in diminishing risks and that it would be more practicable. In answer to the second question Lindahl comes down definitely in favour of an independent standard. His main reason—and it deserves careful consideration—is that the advantages of stable exchange rates are more than counterbalanced by the fact that the movements in a country's price level dictated by the international standard may well be in direct conflict with the requirement that the price level should vary inversely with productivity in that country. Most of the monetary measures which Lindahl discusses can only be applied in a country with a free standard.

It is impossible here to give an adequate idea of the careful and well-balanced way in which Lindahl works out his thesis. We must confine ourselves to one or two particular cases. He uses the concepts of income, profits, and losses to which we have already drawn attention. Assuming a succession of very short equilibrium periods making up a dynamic process, he proceeds to study the price relationships between these periods on different assumptions regarding producers' anticipations at the outset. The introduction of the factor of expectations makes it possible to clear up old difficulties only to bring new ones into view.

For instance, the old problem of the cumulative process which worried Wicksell, Davidson, and Cassel can be satisfactorily settled by applying Lindahl's methods. Taking a closed system in equilibrium, we postulate one primary change, namely, a lowering of the money rate of interest. The result will depend on what we assume about people's expectations regarding the general level of commodity prices. Let us suppose that they expect the prevailing level to be maintained in the future. The fall in the rate of interest will induce a shift of resources from short to long processes ; but this must gradually come to an end, for, as this transference goes on, the marginal productivity of the new investments will decline until it coincides with the lower loan rate of interest. During this process the price level will have risen, but when the new capital goods mature into consumption goods, a further rise will be checked. Investment will be limited to replacement of capital. Assuming no saving (positive or negative) and no other changes in data, a new equilibrium is reached which is different from the starting-point in that there is a greater volume of capital, a higher general price level, and a lower rate of interest. If, alternatively, we assume that people expect the price level, once it begins rising, to continue upwards, then our conclusions will be different. The transference of resources to long processes will be much more marked, because the expected profit in terms of consumption goods at a future date, even allowing for risk, will be greater than is warranted by the lower rate of interest. Accordingly, the rise in the price level will be cumulative : there will be no inherent tendency, as in the first case, to a new equilibrium.

The effects of changes in productivity are emphasized. To illustrate the way in which Lindahl's methods are valuable for this problem, we will take a particular case. First, we assume that the Central Bank decides to regulate the price level so that it will vary inversely with productivity and that individuals foresee the effects of this on future commodity prices. Then suppose that there is a general reduction in costs in the capital goods industries. There is no reason to believe that the price level of final output will fall automatically so that total money income, other things being equal, will remain constant. The first effect of the change in productivity, if there is no change in the rate of interest, is to make long-term investment more profitable. This will immediately curtail the supply of consumption goods and will lead to a rise in their price level, for mobile resources will have moved from direct production of final goods to long period investment. Such a course of events conflicts with the Bank's policy which requires that the price level of consumption goods should first continue unchanged and later fall in proportion to the larger final output due to higher productivity. It is also likely that the redistribution of income will affect the rate of saving. It is, therefore, not true that the monetary authority can afford in this case to be passive while commodity prices fall automatically with lower costs. To correct a state of affairs where long period investment has become relatively more remunerative and saving has not correspondingly increased, the rate of interest should be raised.

If entrepreneurs are inaccurate in estimating the effect on future prices, there will be changes in income and the price level. The producers of capital goods may be over-optimistic and producers of goods not directly affected by the rise in productivity may also miscalculate. If the increase in total income is not offset by increased saving, the demand for final goods will be affected and the price level might even rise. The rate of interest must be used to counteract such tendencies.

All these possibilities may make themselves felt in the transition period before the rise in productivity has had time to increase the output of consumption goods; and therefore, on the above assumptions, the Bank would have to be active during such periods to keep money income constant. As soon as the more productive capital goods have matured into a larger volume of consumers' goods, the price level will fall automatically.

The fact that the goal of Bank policy is made officially known tends to make entrepreneurs behave in such a way as to facilitate its realization. Lindahl has much to say about the proper use of the instruments of policy at the disposal of the Central Bank. Variation of short term interest rates has often to be accompanied by other measures. The long term rate should stand in such a relation to short term rates that the interest cost for a series of short loans should be equal to that of a long loan over a given period of time. If the public miscalculates the future trend, its error will reveal itself in a too low or too high long term rate; and the Central Bank must, therefore, sell or buy securities to counteract it. It may be necessary to differentiate between different rates of interest, e.g. long and short. More important, if it were practicable, would be discrimination according to the use made of borrowed money. We have already discussed the possibilities of such a policy, if it had been adopted during the War-time inflation. Finally, much can be expected from a co-ordination of budgetary measures with monetary policy.

Dropping the assumption of a closed system makes an important difference to the argument. For example, if there is a fall in the costs of producing consumers' goods for export, the effect of the larger output on the price level will not be the same as in a closed system. A rise in productivity may lead to a higher price level, if the larger output is offset by an expansion of exports or a decrease in imports, and if the tendency of the rise in the external value of the currency to lower prices is more than counterbalanced by the internal expansion resulting from the higher incomes of producers.[1] Lindahl carefully analyses the monetary measures required to maintain either a stable price level or a price level varying inversely with productivity in a country on a free standard, given changes in demand for consumption goods, quantitative changes in factors of production, and variations in productivity.[2] He concludes that trade relations with other countries facilitate the regulation of the price level according to a fixed principle of policy when the changes originate inside the country, because the simultaneous movement of the exchange rate assists the monetary authority in carrying out its task. It is much more difficult when an outside change calls for monetary measures not required by the internal situation.

(5) Criticism of the Normal Rate of Interest

In working out his theory of monetary policy Lindahl rejects Wicksell's notion of a normal rate of interest.[3] It will be remembered that in Wicksell's theory the money rate of interest is normal when it corresponds to (*a*) the marginal (physical) rate of return on capital,

[1] See *Penningpolitikens medel*, pp. 163–4.
[2] Ibid., p. 160.
[3] Ibid., pp. 121–134.

(*b*) the rate of interest which equalizes the supply and demand of savings on the capital market, and (*c*) the rate which is neutral in its effect on the price level, i.e. tending neither to raise nor lower it. It is easy to show that one rate cannot do these three things at once. Lindahl objects on the ground that the idea of a " real " rate of return on capital in the physical sense is acceptable only on very abstract assumptions, namely, that there is only one factor of production (apart from waiting) and that this and the product are homogeneous. One can then speak of a " natural rate " in the sense of a relation between produced and invested physical units—a proportion which would vary directly with the period of waiting. But when production involves the use of other scarce factors, it is impossible to express the product and the invested resources in the same units. One must invoke the price mechanism which reflects exchange values. The rate of return ceases to be " real " or technical, for it can only be expressed in terms of prices and is therefore not independent of the rate of interest.[1]

Lindahl puts the essence of his criticism in the following words : " The real rate during a given period can be expressed as the relation between the expected value of future products

[1] This is *a fortiori* true when there are two products instead of one.

(corrected to allow for risk) and the value of the inputs during the period. The price of the invested resources is influenced by the entrepreneurs' demand and this demand is in turn affected by the level of the loan rate of interest. If the money rate is low, the demand for resources to be invested in real capital rises to the point where the investments yield a return corresponding to the loan rate. A high money rate lowers the prices of investment goods, so that their yield again corresponds to the loan rate. We therefore find that the real rate of return on capital has a tendency to adapt itself to the loan rate of interest in each period. The fact that the real rate and the loan rate are equal during any period is no reason for calling the latter normal." [1]

Under dynamic assumptions, it is then argued, the " normal " rate of interest varies with the general expectation regarding the future course of the price level. If 5 per cent is " normal " when everybody expects the ruling price level to remain unchanged, the normal rate becomes 7 per cent when the price level is expected to rise by 2 per cent per annum.

With these criticisms in mind we may pass on to Professor Myrdal's important work on *The Concept of Monetary Equilibrium.* Myrdal does not agree with Lindahl's objections and he insists that the real rate of interest can be

[1] Ibid., p. 124.

defined in such a way that it takes its place as an independent factor in monetary equilibrium. Nevertheless one must not minimize the underlying affinity between the work of these two economists. No higher tribute could be paid to the quality of Lindahl's work than Myrdal's words: "As readers acquainted with the problem under examination will easily see, I have learnt more from Lindahl's *Penningpolitikens medel* than from any other modern work." [1]

(6) The Concept of Monetary Equilibrium

The theory of the natural rate of interest was one of the achievements of the pre-War era in Swedish economic thought. Myrdal's analysis of monetary equilibrium shows that Wicksell's ideas must be completely reinterpreted if they are to be a part of economic dynamics. [2] This essay is a difficult piece of reasoning which cannot be adequately summarized. It is built upon his previous study of "Equilibrium Theory and Change" [3]; and those who cannot read the Swedish book must find the sequel to it rather complicated. All that can be done here is to present a simplified version of the argument and some of the conclusions.

[1] G. Myrdal, "Om penningteoretisk jämvikt," *E.T.*, 1931, p. 193.

[2] G. Myrdal, "Der Gleichgewichtsbegriff als Instrument der geldtheoretischen Analyse," *Beiträge zur Geldtheorie* (edited by F. Hayek), 1934.

[3] *Prisbildningsproblemet och föränderligheten.*

In *Geldzins und Güterpreise* Wicksell used a striking analogy to show the difference between the static equilibrium of relative prices and the equilibrium of money prices. He compared the former with a pendulum which, if disturbed, will oscillate until it again comes to rest. But a system using money resembles a cylinder on a flat surface; under the influence of a given force, it will roll in one direction and there will be no tendency for it to come back to its original resting place.[1] Here we have the idea of the "cumulative process". When an individual invests, he compares the expected rate of return with the price he must pay for the borrowed capital. Imagine a society where entrepreneurs obtain their capital in the form of foodstuffs, which they pay out in wages, rent, etc.; when the process is completed they repay their loans out of the goods produced. Wicksell argued that in such a case there would be a uniform "natural rate" determined by the supply and demand of "real capital". A money economy is not so simple; but if the loan rate of interest corresponds to the rate which would be established in the absence of money, then equilibrium will be maintained. Money is then a mere veil, and does not itself interfere with the real transactions. When the loan rate of interest is above or below the "natural" rate, there is a tendency for the general price

[1] *Geldzins und Güterpreise* (1898), p. 92.

level to move. Wicksell explained the cumulative process as follows. We assume that the money rate is kept below the " natural " rate with the result that prices rise. " The producer's outlay on raw materials, wages, rents, etc., increases, but at the same time he receives a correspondingly higher price for his product ; he, therefore, finds himself in the same relative position as before prices rose, and could afford to pay the previously ruling rate of interest. If the banks maintain the lower rate, he will be able, and competition will force him, to bid more for the factors of production. The increased demand by workers, owners of means of production, etc., will send up the price level of consumers' goods, and the general price level thus rises further." [1]

Myrdal admits that the relation between the money rate and the natural rate is a significant one ; but he finds Wicksell's theory unsatisfactory. He submits it to a searching test and proves that drastic changes are necessary to make it a logically correct dynamic theory.

The rate of return on capital must be defined not in physical but in value terms. Given the existence of money and an uncertain future, there is no sense in talking about the marginal physical return on capital. Wicksell's natural rate presupposes a barter society ; but the money rate of interest implies a system of

[1] Ibid., p. 80 ff.

credit contracts which is obviously incompatible with barter.[1] If the future is imperfectly foreseen, " it is impossible for relative prices to be independent of the monetary unit of account in which credit contracts are reckoned." The " natural rate " must, therefore, be regarded as the yield on capital investment measured in terms of money ; or the proportion between the net return and the value of the capital.

It is impossible here to do justice to the intricate reasoning which leads up to the final definition.[2] The important point is that, in calculating the net yield, allowance is made for anticipated changes in the future value of the capital. The rate of return is thus computed on a constant capital value, so that it may be consistent with the meaning of interest. It is the profit on new investment which sets the cumulative process in motion. If the entrepreneur finds that his total outlay on resources is smaller than the capitalized value of his future net receipts, there is an incentive for him to invest. We can define the rate of return

[1] As Dr. J. R. Hicks has pointed out, the *numéraire* of the Lausanne equations is a mere abstract unit of account in terms of which the prices of other goods and services are expressed. The whole construction assumes perfect foresight, and consequently there is no demand for cash balances. " The appearance of the use of money is intimately connected with imperfect foresight, and it must therefore be analysed in conjunction with the theory of risk. The velocity of circulation of money is in its most important aspect a function of risk." (" Gleichgewicht und Konjunktur," *Zeitschrift für Nationalökonomie*, 1933, p. 448.)

[2] See *Der Gleichgewichtsbegriff* . . ., pp. 391–409.

on planned investment as the margin of profit obtained when the value of existing capital is greater than its reproduction cost. The condition of monetary equilibrium is that the value of capital should be equal to its reproduction cost. Capital value includes by definition the money rate of interest and the anticipated future net receipts. Strictly speaking, the entrepreneur's expectations must be qualified by reference to his degree of faith in his estimate and his gambling preference.

How are we to discover in practice whether a system is in equilibrium or not? A rough idea of reproduction cost could be got from a weighted index of wages, the prices of machinery, raw materials, land, etc.; and this could be compared with an index of the value of industrial shares. But the difference between value and cost of capital has to be worked out first for each individual undertaking; and then all the differences must be added up. Myrdal suggests that the elasticity of new investment in response to a given margin of profit in each undertaking should be used as weights in finding out the trend in the system as a whole.

The second condition of equilibrium according to Wicksell was that the demand for savings equals the supply. This means equality between saving and the cost of new investment. Myrdal's interpretation of this condition is more logical than Mr. Keynes'.[1] Income depends on anticipations of the future; and Saving is that part of it which is not spent on consumption. It is impossible to ignore the subjective nature of these concepts. In Myrdal's words, " present income, which may either be saved or used to buy consumption goods, is ultimately based on our valuations of the present relatively to the future; and this fact deserves much more attention in trade cycle theory." [2]

Suppose that in a closed system there is equilibrium in the sense of equality between the value and reproduction cost of capital. It is then assumed that the owners of capital have occasion to expect higher incomes in the future; but the Bank raises the rate of interest sufficiently to keep capital values constant. The new expectations mean a rise in the community's total income. Capital values have not risen and therefore there is no incentive to new investment. If people decide to go on consuming the same amount as before, the price level of final goods will be unchanged, and the addition to the community's income will represent new saving.

Is equilibrium possible with increased saving but no additional investment? Myrdal explains that the new saving is invested in the expected rise in the value of capital. Theoretically,

[1] The *Treatise on Money*.
[2] Op. cit., p. 414.

savings are demanded not only for the current production of capital goods but also to meet anticipated increases in the value of existing equipment.

The two conditions of equilibrium may be summed up as follows. When the difference between capital value and reproduction cost is zero, the cost of new investment is equal to the quantity of saving.

If there is equilibrium according to these tests, what does it mean in terms of the general price level? Wicksell thought that it implied stability; but his argument did not survive criticism. Attention must be fixed on the behaviour of different groups of prices; and in a dynamic world they can be graded according to the rapidity with which they react to changes. The analysis has distinguished two fundamental groups of prices, which differ very much in this respect, namely, capital values and the reproduction cost of capital. The wages of certain types of labour and the rents of land are comparatively rigid; but capital values move very easily.

Monetary equilibrium implies certain *relations* between groups of prices; and it is therefore compatible with any absolute level of prices. There is nothing in this theory to support the proposal that the general price level should be stabilized. On the contrary there is every reason to believe that such a policy would sow seeds of disturbance. The essential requirement is that the equilibrium relationships should be maintained with the least possible changes in the inflexible prices. Myrdal would construct an index number in which prices are weighted in proportion to their degree of rigidity and also according to their importance for the volume of investment. Keeping such a " price level " constant would mean something quite different from stabilizing the price level of final output or of goods in general. Myrdal has no illusions about the practical usefulness of his construction. He realizes that the notion of the rapidity with which a price responds to a given change is very difficult to define in concrete terms. This " elasticity of reaction varies in the short and long run, in different phases of the trade cycle, and according to the nature of the impulse. It also depends on the character of anticipations ".[1] This is one of the most important problems of dynamic theory. Here is a field where pure analysis will not get very far without the aid of empirical research. There is an urgent need for a body of statistical facts about the way different prices react, and the circumstances influencing the mobility of labour. Even if static theory can do without realistic studies, economic dynamics certainly cannot.

The bearing of this analysis on problems of

[1] Ibid., p. 441.

policy may now briefly be considered. We start from the hypothesis that it is desirable to smooth out cyclical fluctuations, and that this will be achieved if the above-mentioned conditions of equilibrium are maintained. The most important instrument of monetary policy is the discount rate; but the rate of interest on loans is not necessarily a correct indication of the cost of borrowing. This is determined by a bundle of credit conditions of which the interest rate itself is only a part. There is in practice, as Mr. Keynes pointed out, a " fringe of unsatisfied borrowers ". The banks assess the risks associated with different loans and vary their conditions accordingly. The volume of bank credit does not depend only on the rate of interest. We may overlook this fact by assuming a " standard combination " of credit conditions. The question then is: what is the influence of an increase or a decrease in the cost of borrowing on monetary equilibrium? Are there any factors which act as a check on the tendency to a cumulative depression or boom?

Let us assume that credit conditions are stiffened in a closed system. The first result is that the value of capital falls relatively to its reproduction cost; and the rate of investment will decline. Incomes are diminished, first in the constructional industries, and later in the industries producing consumption goods. The shrinkage in the demand for final goods leads to a further decline in capital values ; and thus the downward movement becomes cumulative. This process involves a drastic redistribution of income which probably lowers the rate of saving. This is all the more significant in view of the social institutions of the modern industrial community. Unemployment insurance, rigid wage contracts, and public works tend to check the fall in the price level of consumption goods. Moreover, there are a large number of people, particularly in the middle classes, who will consume their savings rather than suffer a reduction in their standard of living. Directors of companies also like to declare a dividend even though it is not warranted by current profits. The result of all this is that the rate of saving decreases more than total income. In other words the price level of consumers' goods is higher than would otherwise be the case. Capital values fluctuate in sympathy with the anticipated prices of consumers' goods ; and this gives momentum to the cumulative process. But since the redistribution of income helps to maintain the demand for consumption goods, the gap between entrepreneurs' anticipations and their realized net receipts is not as wide as it might have been. Myrdal concludes that, if the forces hindering the fall of the prices of consumers' goods are strong and if the impact of the disappearance of profits on the rate of investment is weak, the effects of banking policy may be neutralized. Thus, in spite of the stiffening of credit conditions, a new equilibrium would be reached with the following characteristics. A more or less unchanged price level of consumption goods, a fall in capital values corresponding to the rise in the rate of interest, lower wages, and a smaller output more particularly in the investment industries, a diminished rate of saving, a shorter average period of investment, and savings equal to investment.[1]

This reasoning is so different from the so-called Austrian Theory of the trade cycle that, to those who hold this theory, it will sound like heresy. It acquits the modern system of social services of being the villain of the piece. It even raises the interesting question whether the absence of such social institutions in the United States helps to account for the peculiar severity of the recent depression in that country. The difference lies in the fact that Myrdal recognizes the essentially dynamic nature of the problem, and does not accept the theory of the capitalistic structure of production which ignores the part played by anticipations.

(7) Conclusion

We have confined this study to the recent contributions of the two leading monetary

[1] Ibid., chapter vii.

theorists of Sweden.[1] Lindahl's work is notable for the clear way in which he distinguishes between the effects of perfect and imperfect foresight. He proves that the consequences of changes in the rate of interest vary according to what is assumed about producers' expectations. The results are qualified by admitting the existence of unemployed labour and capital. A further realistic touch is added when he drops the notion of a single rate of interest and explores the possibilities of discriminating between different uses of credit.

The policy suggested is that the price level should vary inversely with productivity. But he gives no satisfactory indication as to how "general productivity" is to be measured. Costs will not be reduced to the same extent in all industries. Is it certain that the commodities most affected by the new methods will fall in price correspondingly? The idea of a "general change in productivity" is open to the same objections as the "average price level". As it stands it cannot be used as a guide for practical policy.

[1] Unfortunately no account can be given of the works of Professor Ohlin, Dr. D. Hammarskjöld and Dr. J. Åkerman owing to considerations of space. The text does not deal exhaustively with the development of Swedish monetary theory since Wicksell. Particular reference should be made to Ohlin, "Till frågan om penningteoriens upplägning" *E.T.*, 1933, pp. 45–81, and *Penningpolitik, offentliga arbeten, subventioner och tullar som medel mot arbetslöshet* (1934); Dr. Hammarskjöld, "Utkast till en algebraisk metod för dynamisk prisanalys," *E.T.*, 1932, pp. 157–176, and *Konjunkturspridningen* (1933); Dr. J. Åkerman, *Konjunkturteoretiska problem* (1934).

Myrdal's theory of monetary equilibrium is a considerable achievement. He has worked out to their logical conclusion the ideas suggested by Wicksell. The definition of the scope of economic dynamics, the new formulation of the "natural rate of interest", and the analysis of risk and the cumulative element in the trade cycle are valuable additions to knowledge.

Myrdal is very anxious that pure theory should not be a mere exercise in logic, without any connection with the real world. It must be capable of being translated into quantitative terms. He has no use for empty boxes which cannot be filled. But it is the peculiarity of dynamic theory that it rests on individuals' anticipations. How is one to obtain a statistical picture? The ingenious suggestions in Myrdal's essay will not bear examination. It is here that research into the problems of business administration will be of immense value. Systematic studies of the actual policies pursued by business concerns in different phases of the trade cycle must go hand in hand with the development of economic dynamics.

Brief reference may be made to other weaknesses in the theory. In order to apply his equilibrium conditions to the whole system, Myrdal is obliged to work out a very unsatisfactory formula by which the differences between capital value and construction cost may be added up. He seems to be unaware of the fact that this very process of summation smooths out real differences which often contain the germs of disequilibrium. The task of discovering the proper weights to be used in this addition is a purely formal exercise. It actually conceals the important distinction between long and short processes of investment. The significance of a given difference between construction cost and capital value varies according to whether it occurs in firms near to or remote from the stage producing consumption goods.

Myrdal has also failed to take into account the part played by consumers' expectations regarding the placing of their demand for goods and services over the future period of time. His concept of planned voluntary saving does not adequately cover this phenomenon. What is required at the moment of dynamic equilibrium is that the producers' plans regarding investment should synchronize with consumers' decisions regarding the distribution of their demands for final output over the revelant future period. Is it not possible that anticipated saving and investment in Myrdal's sense may be equal at a moment of time, and yet the consumers' expectations and estimates of risk may involve such a spread of expenditure over time as to make disequilibrium inevitable ? The longer the " economic period " the more important is the fact of uncertainty. In the words of Dr. Rosenstein-Rodan, " the presence of this uncertainty factor is essential to every system of economic wants. It is of fundamental importance not only for the planning of production but also for the planning of consumption. The more remote the period planned for, the greater the proportion of wants which can only be estimated for *en bloc*. The risk factor becomes so great that it is impossible to obtain an isolated idea of particular wants." [1] It will now be generally agreed that the real problem concerns the distribution through time of expenditure on consumption goods and the rate at which final output is to become available.

Finally, certain ambiguities must be cleared up before the method of Myrdal's analysis can establish itself securely.[2] An upward or downward movement of the wholesale price level is quite consistent with the maintenance of the equilibrium relationships. He insists that the concept is an instrument designed to show whether there is a cumulative tendency away from equilibrium in either direction. In the light of our previous criticisms, we feel justified in doubting whether the fundamental conditions as defined by Myrdal *necessarily* rule out forces making for a crisis. Dr. J. R. Hicks puts a query in the following words: " . . . what is

[1] "The Role of Time in Economic Theory," *Economica*, February, 1934, pp. 82–3.

[2] An important critical analysis of Myrdal's theory is to be found in Dr. Dag Hammarskjöld's article, "Utkast till en algebraisk metod för dynamisk prisanalys," *E.T.*, 1932, pp. 157–176.

the point of Professor Myrdal's monetary equilibrium ? Certainly not to attain any particular end which he himself regards as socially desirable ; he is very careful to explain this. The only clue which he gives is a reference back to Wicksell—that monetary disequilibrium implies the setting in of a ' Wicksellian cumulative process '. But, at the stage he has reached, has he the right to refer back to Wicksell any longer ? Just what is the precise difference between such a cumulative process and the sort of inflation which he would consider, theoretically at least, as consistent with monetary equilibrium ? "[1] The ultimate bearing of the theory on the problems of policy will depend on the answers to these questions.

The foregoing study of monetary equilibrium, in so far as it bears on the trade cycle, is in quite a different category from Dr. Hayek's theory. No use is made of the " average period of production " ; the explanation of the crisis after an inflation as necessarily due to scarcity of capital is rejected ; and stress is laid on the cumulative nature of the boom and the slump.

Professors Mises and Hayek, though deeply distrusting the idea of an average price level, have made the concept of the " average period of production " the corner-stone of their theory of fluctuations. It is very doubtful whether

[1] Review of *Beiträge zur Geldtheorie*, *Economica*, November, 1934, p. 483.

the movements of this arbitrarily defined average correspond to anything in the real world. There is not even the prospect that more abundant statistics will one day fill this empty box. The idea is important in the static theory of capital; but it has serious limitations in dynamic analysis.[1]

According to Dr. Hayek, " the task of Trade Cycle theory is to show under what conditions a break may occur in that tendency towards equilibrium which is described in pure analysis —i.e. why prices, in contradiction to the conclusions of static theory, do not bring about such changes in the quantities produced as would correspond to an equilibrium situation."[2] This statement of the problem should have been accompanied by a definition of what is meant by dynamic as distinct from static theory. Until this has been done, the trade cycle theorist has no firm ground under his feet. Economic dynamics, as Myrdal has shown, analyses the price system under the influence of uncertainty; and, therefore, if the term " equilibrium " is used in this context it must mean something other than static equilibrium. How different Dr. Hayek's approach is may be illustrated by the following quotation: " If we want to explain fluctuations of production, we

[1] Cf. E. Schneider, " Das Zeitmoment in der Theorie der Produktion," Part I, *Jahrbücher für Nationalökonomie und Statistik*, 1935, p. 271 ff.

[2] *Monetary Theory and the Trade Cycle*, pp. 70–1.

have to give a complete explanation . . . we have to start where general economic theory stops ; that is to say at a condition of equilibrium when no unused resources exist. The existence of such unused resources is itself a fact which needs explanation. It is not explained by static analysis and, accordingly, we are not entitled to take it for granted. . . . It is my conviction that if we want to explain economic phenomena at all, we have no means available but to build on the foundations given by the concept of a tendency towards an equilibrium." [1] We have seen that it is legitimate and necessary in dynamic theory to assume unused resources ; and if Dr. Hayek had done this, he would have had to alter some of his conclusions. A theory of policy based on the assumption of full employment is incomplete and even dangerous.

One of the chief shortcomings of *Prices and Production* is that it does not recognize the importance of expectations and risk. In fact Dr. Hayek makes use of the assumption of perfect foresight to support a vital part of his argument. The thesis is that an increase in saving must necessarily lead to a lengthening of the structure of production and a change in relative prices which will constitute a new equilibrium. The following sentences are worth noting : " Only at a lower rate of interest than that formerly prevailing will it be possible

[1] *Prices and Production* (2nd ed.), p. 34.

to lend these funds (the new savings), and how far the rate of interest will fall will depend upon the amount of the additional funds and the *expectation of profits on the part of entrepreneurs* willing to expand their production. *If these entrepreneurs entertain correct views about the price changes which are to be expected as a result of the changes in the method of production*, the new rate of interest should correspond to the system of price margins which will ultimately be established. In this way, from the outset, the use of the additional funds which have become available will be confined to those entrepreneurs who hope to obtain the highest profits out of their use, and all extensions of production, for which the additional funds would not be sufficient, will be excluded." [1] This conclusion must obviously be modified as soon as one makes the reasonable assumption that entrepreneurs have incorrect views about future price changes. The method of economic dynamics is to analyse the probable course of events on different assumptions relating to producers' expectations. The hypothesis that they enjoy perfect foresight is ruled out altogether.

There is another weak link in Dr. Hayek's chain of argument. The injection of new money leads to a lengthening of the structure of production and a rise in prices, particularly

[1] *Prices and Production* (2nd ed.), pp. 84–5 (italics are mine).

in the capital goods industries. "Forced savings" are extorted from consumers: in other words they get less commodities for their money. According to Dr. Hayek, "there can be no doubt that, if their money receipts should rise again, they would immediately attempt to expand consumption to the usual proportion." [1] When this happens, the prices of consumers' goods rise suddenly—an indication of the scarcity of capital—and this brings on the crisis. It is taken for granted that the increase in the volume of money has no effect on people's ability and willingness to save. This assumption is quite untenable. During the early stage of a boom there is a redistribution of income which on balance increases the rate of saving, just as in the first part of a depression there is a fall in the rate of saving. Up to a certain point, the upward swing of the trade cycle is supported by an increase in voluntary saving; and it is only when this point has been passed that the boom becomes unsound. On the other hand, the early phase of a depression is a necessary process of liquidation; but, since the slump is cumulative, it may go on further than is necessary. A wasteful secondary deflation may result from an all-round reduction in wages at a time when producers' expectations are very gloomy. Dr. Hayek is not justified in issuing the grim warning that "we can do

[1] Hayek, op. cit., p. 57.

nothing to get out of a depression before its natural end ".[1]

In a recent article Dr. Hayek has admitted the importance of anticipations in trade cycle theory.[2] He seeks to reveal the assumptions about foresight which underlie the argument in *Prices and Production.* Apparently, the reasoning sometimes assumes that entrepreneurs expect existing prices to be maintained in future; at other points, as in the passage quoted above, perfect foresight is postulated. It is doubtful whether the risk factor with all its complications can be made compatible with Dr. Hayek's conception of the structure of production. There are several interesting passages in the above-mentioned article which show that the author is in sympathy with some of the ideas of the Swedish neo-Wicksellian school. For example, " the task is not to construct one theory of the trade cycle, i.e. a detailed scheme which will explain all empirical fluctuations, but to develop that branch of theory which we need for the analysis of the various kinds of fluctuations found in the real world."[3] Dr. Hayek tentatively enumerates certain problems connected with producers' expectations, the solution of which will throw much light on the theory of fluctuations; and

[1] Op. cit., p. 87.

[2] " Preiserwartungen, monetäre Störungen und Fehlinvestitionen," *Nationaløkonomisk Tidsskrift*, 1935.

[3] Ibid., p. 178.

he concludes with a laudatory reference to Myrdal's treatment of the risk factor.

In conclusion, attention must be drawn to another qualification necessary before the concept of monetary equilibrium can serve as a basis for the theory of policy. The revised " natural rate of interest ", defined in terms of value productivity, has definite meaning in a closed system. In Myrdal's terminology one may compare the value of capital with its construction cost. But the " natural rate " in an open system is a function partly of conditions of demand and supply in other countries. It would, therefore, be inconsistent to apply the propositions of the theory of dynamic equilibrium to the situation in an open system, without recognizing these new elements in the problem. Where a group of countries may be said to form parts of a general " structure of production ", international capital movements are akin to the transfer of non-specific resources from stage to stage. But there is no corresponding mobility of labour. When the problem is put in these extreme terms, it is easy to see that the " natural rates " in the various countries are to some degree interdependent, and that measures designed to keep the " money rate " equal to the " natural rate " in any one country do not necessarily guarantee equilibrium.

A complete theory of the business cycle will have to cover at least three different problems :

the irregular occurrence of technical progress; the relation between producers' anticipations and changes in the data; and the nature of the cumulative process.

Economics will be a safe guide to policy only when the theory of dynamics has been fully developed. Judging by the time it has taken for the theory of static equilibrium to receive general assent, we are now only at the beginning of a new stage in the evolution of the science. Since so much depends on how people's expectations react to changes in circumstances, it is not so certain that interference is always an evil. The economist must construct several models of the real world and indicate the probable causal sequence in each. He who seeks light on problems of policy must be careful to select the most appropriate model for the situation which he is examining.

Chapter IV

THEORETICAL ASPECTS OF AN EXPANSIONIST POLICY

THE outstanding feature of recent years has been the attempts made in countries with paper standards to lift themselves from the slough of depression. The breakdown of the international standard gave Governments and Central Banks a great measure of freedom to embark on independent policies ; and the industrial revival experienced in certain countries, particularly those belonging to the sterling *bloc*, is to a large extent due to the use which has been made of this new freedom. The controversy regarding stabilization involves something more than the proper working of the world's monetary system. It is the aim of democratic Socialist Parties no less than Fascist regimes to use the machinery of the State in order to secure full and stable employment of resources ; and ultimately the question arises whether the obligations of belonging to an international monetary club are compatible with these national programmes. In one way it is easier for a corporate state because the dictator seems to be able to adjust the level of real wages by decree. But in democratic countries where Trade Unionism is still strongly entrenched the rigidity of the wage system must be taken as an important datum in the problem. Socialists have always been internationally-minded; but far too little thought has been devoted to the implications of insular socialistic measures.

Adherence to the Labour Party's programme involves full support of the international political organization—the League of Nations—and a refusal to belong to the international monetary organization—the gold standard. Dr. Hugh Dalton, in his authoritative exposition of British Socialist Policy, is unequivocal on these two questions. On the one hand, he declares, "the Labour Party stands with deliberate emphasis and without any shuffling or ambiguity for the Collective Peace System. It stands, in other words, for the honest and energetic fulfilment by this country of all its treaty obligations, including notably the Kellogg Pact and the League Covenant."[1] On the other hand, "Britain kissed gold good-bye, to the horror of our bankers, in September, 1931, and many other countries, including, after an interval of eighteen months, the United States, have followed our example. I hope it is good-bye for ever. . . . Stability of exchange rates is not worth purchasing at too high a price, even

[1] Hugh Dalton, *Practical Socialism for Britain* (1935), p. 367.

for a country whose external trade is so important as that of Britain. It is not worth purchasing at the price of a British return to the gold standard."[1] We may ignore the view of the small minority of the Party which is convinced that adherence to British obligations under the Covenant implies in certain circumstances an acquiescence in Imperialist designs and is therefore incompatible with the Socialist ideal. Socialists will, however, be unanimous in their opposition to a reconstituted gold standard if it makes impossible the achievement of a Labour Government's plans of economic reconstruction. The advent of the second Labour Government in England in 1929, when the country had been struggling for five years with an overvalued currency, was bound to hasten the departure from gold, even if events in the United States and Germany had not precipitated an international crisis. A Socialist Government cannot be expected to bring about drastic cuts in wages in the interests of exchange stability.

A similar reaction against an international standard is discernible in the Scandinavian countries. Labour Governments have been in office in Sweden, Denmark, and Norway during the recent depression, and they are not likely to be in favour of international monetary rules which will restrict the margin necessary

[1] Ibid., pp. 194, 198.

for their future programmes. They are fully aware of the disadvantages of fluctuating exchanges rates and particularly of the dangers of competitive currency depreciation. But they are impressed by the grave risks associated with any attempt to re-establish the post-War gold standard in present conditions ; and, in Sweden at least, people are optimistic that the country can insulate itself from the fluctuations of a chaotic world. In view of this dilemma more than passing interest attaches to the recovery measures recently applied in countries with paper standards. Swedish economists have given careful consideration to the complicated theoretical issues involved ; and, though the problems have been treated from the point of view of a small country, much can be learnt from their conclusions.

It is proposed in this chapter to examine some theoretical aspects of an expansionist policy on various alternative assumptions.

(1) The State and the Economic Order

Before the conclusions of the theory of value can be used as a guide to the real world, it is essential to show that the assumptions of the doctrine bear some kind of resemblance to reality. Recent work on imperfect competition supports a conclusion hinted at by Knut Wicksell before the War, namely, that in certain cases more competition, i.e. the arrival of new entrants in an industry, involves excess capacity, a wastage of resources, and an injury to consumers.[1] Wicksell held that the best remedy would be an association among buyers ; recent analysis suggests compulsory standardization or restriction of entry to enable producers to realize more effectively the " economies of scale ".[2] These examples show that the case against " interference " is not very plausible when some of the unreal assumptions are removed. If this is the moral left by new formulations of static analysis, it is all the more true of the results obtained in economic dynamics. A theory which recognizes the role of expectations of an uncertain future makes the dogma of non-interference most unreasonable. If we accept the view that the risks due to imperfect foresight ought to be reduced, it is clear that there are numerous possibilities of State intervention which will do more good than harm.

Industrial fluctuations are apt to be cumulative. The task of the economist is to distinguish various assumptions and to indicate the policies which would exercise a moderating effect in each case. He should not confine himself to one particular model of the economic system and

[1] See K. Wicksell, *Lectures*, vol. i, pp. 87–8 ; E. Chamberlin *The Theory of Monopolistic Competition*, chapter v ; N. Kaldor " Market Imperfection and Excess Capacity," *Economica* February, 1935, pp. 33–50.

[2] Cf. N. Kaldor, loc. cit.

conclude that the Government ought to do as little as possible.

One of the serious gaps in economic analysis is the failure to incorporate an adequate theory of the State. The notion that taxes resemble slugs which batten on the fruits of the garden dies hard in many quarters. Nothing is more obvious than the fact that the State is a necessary part of the economic order. We may distinguish three functions. In so far as the State is a buyer and seller of private resources it is on the same footing as any other economic subject. The State (and the same applies to municipal authorities) is also a producer of " public goods " which satisfy consumers' " collective wants ". Here is a significant exchange relationship. Thirdly, the Government, as the instrument of the compulsory political association, passes legislation the purpose of which is to modify the legal and social framework within which economic activity takes place. The second and third functions overlap to some extent ; but there remains a vital distinction.

De Viti de Marco, who has made an important contribution to the economic theory of the State, defines collective wants as those which have their sole origin in the fact that individuals live together in a community.[1] The public goods which are produced by the State in order

[1] A. de Viti de Marco, *I primi principii dell' economia finanziaria*, chapter i.

to satisfy these wants are often such that they cannot be split up into consumption units. There is no means of finding out the amount consumed by the individual buyer. This is the case with roads in a modern country; but was not true of roads under the turnpike system. The problem of public finance, as formulated by modern theorists,[1] is the transformation of private resources into public goods. A significant change in data takes place when a majority of individuals decide to allocate more of their income for the purchase of public goods and less for private goods. This is met by an extension of certain kinds of public enterprise. Recent decades have witnessed a profound alteration in individual valuations in this direction; and economists have been very slow in adjusting their technique to the intricate problems created thereby.

The attempts made to tackle this question have not perhaps inspired much confidence. The collective nature of public goods is responsible for substantial differences between the consumer's valuations in the individualistic and the public sphere. It is not easy for a person to decide the precise advantage he stands to gain from public goods. He may be influenced either because he takes into account their utility to other people or on account of his

[1] e.g. De Viti de Marco, op. cit., and Erik Lindahl, *Die Gerechtigkeit der Besteuerung*.

conviction that in a class society it is possible for one section to benefit at the expense of another.

If the majority in a democratic community want more hospitals, parks, and nursery schools, public enterprise will expand in response to these preferences. But the classes who get most benefit from these services do not have to go without private goods in order to meet the expense. Theoretically a tax is the price paid by the citizen for the portion of the public services which he consumes. Taxes are compulsory and are levied according to the individual's ability to pay as measured, for instance, by his income or the value of his property. The cost of public goods demanded by one class may, thus, fall largely on other classes. Social legislation is to a great extent a method of enabling the poorer classes to obtain public goods below cost price.

The third function of the State, namely, the modification of the legal and social framework, may also be interpreted as a response to certain preferences which do not express themselves in the usual monetary scale,[1] e.g. a demand for security or for the maintenance of health or æsthetic standards. Changes in the social data have important economic reactions: they may or may not tend to aggravate the instability of the economic order.

[1] Cf. E. F. M. Durbin, " The Social Significance of the Theory of Value," *Economic Journal*, December, 1935.

The propositions relating to industrial fluctuations outlined in the previous chapter will serve as a basis for a discussion of the probable effects of various types of interference.

(2) The International Margin

A theory of monetary policy must start from an analysis of a closed system. The results thus obtained, though of fundamental importance, are not necessarily applicable to a country which is closely bound up with the rest of the world. The actual problem is most frequently that of an open system; and it is not sufficient merely to show what measures are suitable for a closed system and then add a corollary that these can only succeed if the country is on an independent paper standard. Each step in the theory of policy must take into account the reactions of different measures on the balance of payments. It is idle to underestimate the extreme difficulty of such a task. In this chapter a very sketchy attempt will be made to indicate some of the problems involved.

We shall begin by assuming a country on an independent paper standard in the trough of a depression seeking to absorb unused factors of production into employment. Such a starting point might strike a trade cycle theorist as being question-begging. He might ask: what does the phrase "trough of a depression" mean? He might object that, if it implies that a drastic process of liquidations has paved the way for a spontaneous revival of investment, the best thing the authorities can do is to allow nature to complete the cure. To meet this argument it is sufficient to assume that the system is at a stage of the downward swing (i.e. falling production, employment, and real income) where further cost-reducing measures would precipitate a cumulative secondary deflation.[1] There is a considerable volume of unused resources particularly in capital goods industries. Though the price level of consumption goods has not fallen as much as that of capital goods, entrepreneurs responsible for real investment expect prices to go on falling. The country's international trade has suffered a substantial shrinkage. By crisis policy we mean a combination of measures relating to credit conditions, public finance, wages, and tariffs calculated to prevent the secondary deflation and induce a rise in production, real income, and the level of employment. The object of the analysis will be to examine the effects of each of these measures taken separately.

The price and income structure of the country is susceptible to the influence of internal measures and of external fluctuations on the balance of payments. An independent policy,

[1] Cf. Röpke, "Die sekundäre Krise und ihre Überwindung," *Essays in Honour of Gustav Cassel* (1933), pp. 557–568.

therefore, presupposes an "international margin" supplied by a favourable foreign balance. A recovery measure will influence the balance of payments by way of physical imports and exports or of capital movements or of both. For instance a public works programme will tend to increase imports relatively to exports and, in view of the consequent adverse balance, the authorities might have to choose between checking the incipient recovery or acquiescing in a further fall in the external value of the currency. There is, then, in any given situation a limit beyond which expansionist measures cannot go without reacting unfavourably on the balance of payments. The limit is, of course, more or less elastic, and some of the measures have the effect of pushing it further away.[1]

The international margin tends to be widened in the following circumstances:—

(1) Where there is a favourable shift in the foreign demand for the country's exports.

(2) When foreign capital flows into the country.

(3) The greater the fall in the external value of the currency which can be safely allowed.

(4) The greater the proportion of the increased income due to internal expansion which is saved.

[1] Cf. G. Myrdal, *Konjunktur och offentliga hushållning* (1933), p. 27 ff.

(5) The less susceptible imports and exports are to variations in the internal income and price level.

(6) The greater the proportion of the rising volume of internal production and consumption which results in a demand for home-produced goods.

(7) The greater the reduction in its foreign exchange reserve which the Central Bank can contemplate.

The measures which tend to create or widen a positive foreign balance may be divided into three categories.[1]

(*a*) Those which not only widen the international margin but also have a stimulating effect on internal business conditions, e.g. moderate currency depreciation, import duties, and export premiums.

(*b*) Those which are neutral in their effect on internal business conditions, e.g. increased capital imports or diminished capital exports (direct measures with this end in view might, however, lead to a loss of confidence), cuts in wages which benefit some employers by reducing their costs but injure others by lowering the demand for consumers' goods.

(*c*) Those which have a depressing effect on internal business conditions, e.g. higher taxation which diminishes the demand for consumers'

[1] See Myrdal, *Finanspolitikens ekonomiska verkningar* (1934), pp. 269–270.

goods, cuts in wages paid by the State and public bodies, other economies which are not counter-balanced by measures reducing saving.

Professor Myrdal argues that, unless there are strong reasons to the contrary, the first category should be preferred to the second, and the second to the third. This classification is of some interest ; but it presupposes a more exact knowledge of the incidence of the measures within each category than is attainable. There is no precise line of demarcation, though it is useful to contrast the effect of a certain amount of currency depreciation on the one hand with that of an all round reduction in wages in public employment on the other. Each of these measures will widen the margin ; but it is clear that the former alone will, *ceteris paribus*, be certain to expand business activity.

If the international margin is relatively narrow, the question arises as to how best to utilize it. What combination of measures will achieve the greatest stimulus ? The authorities will be faced with a choice between various alternatives, e.g. between cheap money and State expenditure, or, assuming the latter is chosen, between different methods of financing public investment. The more orthodox view is that credit policy should be given preference over budgetary measures. It is questionable whether, in the case of a country in the situation above described, such a choice is advantageous. The discount rate may have to be reduced so low that the banks will feel an undue strain. In a country like Sweden, where it is difficult to get the savings banks to fall into line, the commercial banks are likely to be deterred from reducing their loan rate below a reasonable level. Moreover, if there is an effective international capital market and an absence of abnormal risk, a fall in the rate of interest might lead to an export of capital which would tend to curtail the international margin. Another point of importance is that the expectations of entrepreneurs may be so pessimistic that no amount of reduction in the money rate of interest will be sufficient to induce them to embark on new investment. A judicious use of the instrument of credit discrimination might get over some of these difficulties. Nevertheless, there are strong reasons for believing that public investment is the surer way of utilizing a restricted international margin.

Generally speaking, one country's international margin can only be widened at the expense of that of other countries. Mr. Keynes has been careful to point out that " improving the foreign balance so that a larger proportion of current expenditure again becomes income in the hands of home producers . . . merely means that one country is withdrawing employment and spending power from the rest of the world. For when one country improves its foreign balance, it follows that the foreign balance of some other country is diminished . . . competitive currency depreciations and competitive tariffs, and more artificial means of improving an individual country's foreign balance such as exchange restrictions, import prohibitions, and quotas, help no one and injure each, if they are applied all round ".[1] Nevertheless, it is pertinent to note that the phrase " at the expense of the rest of the world " must be interpreted with due regard to the position of the country in question. If the country's currency has been obviously overvalued for some years, a policy of depreciation will up to a point be a legitimate means of widening its international margin. This factor is relevant in the explanation of Britain's recovery in the years 1932–5. One cannot accuse a country of sponging on the rest of the world if it is merely adjusting the external value of its currency to the point compatible with the new relation between its price and income structure and that of other countries. Furthermore, when a large country is creating a favourable foreign balance for the purpose of inducing internal recovery, it is necessary to distinguish between short-run and long-run consequences. In the short-run the rest of the world may well be impoverished. But, assuming that the measures made possible by the

[1] J. M. Keynes, *The Means to Prosperity* (1933), pp. 18–19.

artificially created international margin bring about a substantial rise in the country's production, real income, and prices, the favourable reactions communicated to the rest of the world will more than compensate for the previous short-run impoverishment. The beneficial effects secured in this way will be greater, the larger the country in question, the closer its commercial relations with the rest of the world and the more susceptible other countries are to external stimuli. This argument has some bearing on the recovery measures in the United States.

Finally, the scope for an internal expansion may be widened by an increase in the foreign demand for a country's exports. The elbow-room thus afforded can become the basis for an upswing which need not threaten the stability of the external value of the currency. For example, Sweden experienced a favourable change in the demand for her exports in the 'twenties ; but her internal boom was tempered by the fact that the margin was used up through a large export of capital. The rapid improvement in the foreign demand for Swedish products since 1933 has given the country a unique opportunity of pursuing an independent policy.

(3) Public Investment and Sound Finance

Before proceeding with the analysis of the utilization of a given international margin by means of a policy of public investment, it is necessary to consider the question of its bearing on " sound finance ". Discussions of public works as a method of overcoming depression usually concentrate on the short-run effects. Very little attention has been given to the long-run aspects. An extension of Government expenditure financed by loans generally means unbalancing the budget in any one year. But from the point of view of policy, the fact that the national accounts are drawn up on an annual basis is an accident. The financial purist is certain to regard as unorthodox any extraordinary outlay on State investments which involves a current deficit. The idea of " sound finance " is, however, a long-run conception. There is no reason why the value of State assets should not remain constant over a long period, although in certain years the budget may be " under-balanced ". Long-run soundness is guaranteed if the deficits of the lean years are fully compensated by the surpluses of the fat years. The use of the budget as the handmaiden of credit policy must be part of a long-run financial plan which at least maintains the value of the national assets constant.

That the technical problem is capable of solution may be shown by reference to the budgetary system of Denmark.[1] Since the

[1] See K. Müller, " Die Neugestaltung des staatlichen Rechnungs- und Revisionswesens in Dänemark," *Finanz-Archiv*, 1928, pp. 131–9, and Myrdal, op. cit., pp. 146–158.

reforms of 1927 the financial accounts of that country have been organized in such a way that elastic methods of " balancing " the budget in the short run are combined with long-run guarantees providing for a slow increase in the net value of State assets. There are two separate accounts—the current or ordinary budget and the capital budget. Any outlay which creates a material asset of a durability extending beyond one year belongs to the capital budget. This heading comprises not only investments in public enterprises, the acquisition of shares in semi-public or private undertakings and the granting of loans but also non-self-liquidating expenditure such as the building of schools, hospitals, administrative offices, etc. A unique feature of the Danish system is that the ordinary budget of each branch of administration is debited with the depreciation and interest charge on the durable capital employed in it, whether it be self-liquidating or not. For example, the expenditure estimate for the University of Copenhagen in 1933–4 totalled 4,407,018 kronor: one of the items covered, namely, building expenses, amounted to 1,363,067 kronor which included 900,605 kronor for interest and 201,587 kronor for depreciation.[1] This means that the annual diminution in the value of the capital equipment for every kind used in each branch of

[1] See Myrdal, op. cit., p. 149.

administration is met by a corresponding charge on the total ordinary budget of the country for the year in question. A capital outlay appears first in the capital budget. In the next year it is entered up among the State assets, while the current budget is debited with its depreciation and interest. The depreciation and interest payments are a contribution made by the current budget to the capital budget. They appear in the latter as a credit item corresponding to the liability represented by service of public debt. An aggregate statement is presented annually showing the amount of the national debt and the value of national assets. The difference between Danish and Swedish practice is worthy of notice. In Sweden the ordinary budget is balanced each year in a straightforward manner, and the budget law decrees that capital outlays which do not yield a monetary return must be defrayed out of current revenue. It is only self-liquidating capital expenditure that can be financed by loans in the capital budget. In Denmark, on the other hand, the ordinary budget is not balanced in the usual way. It shows a plus or a minus which is entered in the aggregate closed accounts as an addition to or deduction from the State's net assets. The distinction between " productive " and " non-productive " capital expenditure is of subsidiary importance from the point of view of budget technique. To continue our previous example, the University of Copenhagen in 1933–4 had an estimated income of 418,338 kronor as against its total expenditure (including depreciation and interest) of 4,407,180 kronor. The net outlay of 3,988,680 kronor thus appeared in the Danish ordinary budget.

It is interesting to note that the income side of the capital budget includes not only loans but the proceeds of inheritance taxes. This is partly a recognition of the burdensome incidence of such taxes on saving and partly a means of securing for the capital budget a contribution over and above the ordinary depreciation sums. The fact that the ordinary budget in any year shows a deficit is of small significance. The real situation is registered by the relation between the public debt and the value of the net assets of the State. Flexibility in the short-run is made possible through the long-run guarantee of sound finance implied by the provisions regarding depreciation and interest payments on all capital expenditure coupled with the ear-marking of certain revenues e.g. inheritance taxes. This system has great advantages. The budget can be "underbalanced" in times of depression and thus help to quicken recovery, without any threat to the soundness of the country's finances. The system has been in vogue in Denmark since 1927; and the comparative firmness displayed by Danish bonds on the English and American markets disproves the argument that these unconventional methods of securing budgetary equilibrium injure the country's credit.

Professor Myrdal, in his exhaustive study of the economic effects of public finance, proposes the application of the Danish technique to the Swedish budget.[1] Self-liquidating public investment in Sweden is already administered under what is known as " The State Productive Funds ". The revenues expected from these public enterprises appear in the general budget as net items, arrived at after costs and depreciation charges have been allowed for. The suggestion is that the organization of so-called " non-productive " investment should embody the same principle. Separate departments responsible for non-self-liquidating public works would regularly send in their estimates of incomes and costs (including interest and amortization) ; and the general ordinary budget would be debited with the net items which would of course be negative. The problems raised by the principles governing depreciation and the periodical necessity for writing down the value of certain capital objects, e.g. railways or school buildings, are by no means simple. But the experience of Denmark shows that they are not insuperable. Such a system is

[1] See Myrdal, op. cit., part iii.

indispensable as a logical foundation for any long-term planning of public investment. It is true that it is easier to apply in small countries like Sweden which are in the fortunate position of having State assets whose value considerably exceeds the volume of public debt. Nevertheless, even for large countries like Britain, the United States, or Germany, with quite different budgetary traditions, the technique suggested has much to recommend it. Those who have advocated a capital budget for Great Britain have done the cause an ill service by failing to point out how they propose to protect the integrity of State finances.

This brings us to the important political aspect of this reform. It is one of the disadvantages of a democratic budgetary system that there is no certainty that the future amortization of present " non-productive " expenditure will be carried out. The combination of short-period flexibility with long-run financial integrity inevitably implies removing certain decisions regarding the public purse from the control of future Parliaments. The guardians of liberty will object that the pure gold of democratic control will be debased with the alloy of dictatorship. When the *vox populi* changes the balance of forces in Parliament, the new legislators will find their freedom of action checked by the dead hand of the past. Some economists in authoritarian countries feel justified in calling attention to the obvious superiority of the corporate state over the democratic in this matter.[1] This particular dilemma is not a serious one for a country which prizes liberty as an end and not merely as a means. The freedom of action of the British legislature in regard to finance is already limited in several directions ; and an extension of the principle of ear-marked revenues would not be revolutionary. The larger end is the achievement of economic stability. One of the means necessary for its attainment is the acceptance of long-run commitments ensuring the maintenance of the net value of the State's assets. Though this no doubt enlarges the list of accomplished facts which the freely elected representatives of the people will be unable to amend, it is surely a small price to pay. Here is a case where the end does justify the means.

(4) THE BUDGET, PUBLIC WORKS, AND THE TRADE CYCLE

A depression invariably has the effect of diminishing the yield of taxes and adding to certain items of expenditure, particularly the cost of unemployment relief. The Finance Minister is usually forced to stiffen tax rates, particularly those which are less susceptible than the average to changes in business conditions, as well as to practise rigid economy.

[1] Cf. O. Morgenstern, *Die Grenzen der Wirtschaftspolitik*, p. 130.

He may in this way achieve a balanced budget, but often only at the expense of aggravating the depression. The cumulative downward process is accompanied by a drastic curtailment of investment and frantic attempts by entrepreneurs to secure liquidity. Just at the time when the private industrialists are all practising economy, the Government is compelled by orthodox finance to do the same. When consumers respond to the eloquent appeal that they should economize, they naturally reduce their purchases of consumption goods; but when the State economizes, it cannot help diminishing the volume of public investment. It is impossible to avoid making adjustments in the current revenue and expenditure items when the price level falls, but different measures vary a great deal in their economic impact.

The Chancellor of the Exchequer usually wields his axe on certain types of current or ordinary expenditure. Let us assume that the expenses he deletes could have been financed out of current revenue, and that other expenditures are given, i.e. independent of the item in question. We may thus concentrate on the effects of his financial "saving". Professor Myrdal has distinguished two broad classes of economy: on the one hand, a general reduction in the wages, salaries, etc., paid to public employees without a curtailment of the scope of public employment, on the other, a contraction in the extent of the activities of the Government, e.g. the dismissal of labour. The former may be examined first. The curtailment of expenditure makes it possible to reduce a certain tax or to avoid a stiffening of taxation. It, therefore, involves a transference of income from public servants to the taxpayers. The effects of this redistribution of income on business conditions will depend on the difference between the use made of it by the taxpayers and the use which the public employees would have made of it. It is difficult to be precise but perhaps a rough approximation may be suggested on certain assumptions.[1]

We assume that, in the absence of the Government's saving on its wages bill, a particular tax would have to be stiffened. Now it may be that the cut reduces the consumption and saving of the public servants in the same proportions as the tax would have done in the case of the taxpayers. In that event the transference of income would have hardly any bearing on the course of the depression. There are two qualifications. There might be a horizontal transfer of demand from some categories of consumption goods to others but there would be no net stimulus to the capital goods industries. Assuming, however, that the increase in taxation, if levied, would have

[1] See Myrdal, *Finanspolitikens ekonomiska verkningar*, part iv, chapter ii, for the full statement of this analysis.

borne heavily on people's willingness to invest, the application of the axe would on balance give a net fillip to real investment.

If the tax which is avoided would have curtailed consumption, while the wage cut is offset by an inroad into savings, so that the public servants maintain their demand for consumers' goods, the effect will be a diminution in saving. On the assumption that there is an adequate international margin and that credit for private industry will not be reduced as a result of the fall in saving, we may conclude that the result would be beneficial. On the other hand, if the tax is of the type which would have reduced the taxpayers' saving whereas the loss of wages by the public servants leads to a corresponding diminution in the demand for consumers' goods, the measure will have a detrimental effect. For, on our assumptions regarding entrepreneurs' expectations and their desire to be as liquid as possible, we cannot expect this net addition to savings to result in new investment. A similar analysis would be relevant if the State, instead of reducing the wages of public employees, dismissed a certain number of them. This would probably hit the lower income groups and would therefore be all the more certain to diminish the demand for consumption goods. When it is a question of balancing the budget the weight of argument is in favour of general wage cuts rather than a curtailment of the scope of public employment.

The analysis of the conditions of recovery may now be continued on the assumption that the country's budget is organized according to the principles outlined in the previous section. There can, therefore, be no financial objection to " under-balancing " in the interests of industrial revival. It is here argued that, at the stage of the downward swing which we envisage, a programme of public investment financed out of loans is desirable. The industrial system we have in mind is one in which the State and the municipalities are already considerable producers of public and private goods. The object of a policy of public works is not to increase the permanent scope of State enterprise at the expense of private enterprise. It is rather to supply an indispensable stimulus to the rate of private investment.

The theoretical justification for this argument is to be found in the analysis of Chapter III. The static idea that capital used in one line of investment must necessarily be taken away from some other line does not correspond to what happens in a dynamic situation. The capital necessary for an industrial recovery does not exist as an accumulated stock, but is generated during the upward swing itself.[1]

[1] See Myrdal, op. cit., p. 220 ff.

Nature's cure comes about when private entrepreneurs change their views about the future and begin to invest again. As soon as the tide turns the rise in incomes and their redistribution bring about an automatic increase in the rate of saving. The policy here suggested is simply that the revival of business activity should be induced by a programme of public investment as soon as the depression has liquidated the excesses of the previous boom. Let us ignore the complications of a narrow international margin.

There are considerable unused resources, particularly in the capital producing industries. An increase in demand due to loan-financed State expenditure will mean an addition to the receipts of the owners of capital instruments, even if prices do not rise. A portion of this additional income will be saved. The reabsorbed workers will also save some of their income. Moreover the tendency of companies to pursue a cautious dividend policy when their prospects begin to improve involves an automatic rise in the rate of saving; and the rigidity of consumption habits will work in the same direction. If the stimulus is strong enough it will affect sectional price levels in such a way as to increase capital values, thus creating a positive difference between capital value and reproduction cost and leading to renewed private investment. This is admittedly a simplified version of the process. It is important to remember that liquidations do not necessarily involve abandoning the physical instruments brought into existence in the previous boom. Much of this plant will be started up as soon as anticipations become favourable ; and if such unused capacity is large, the extension of demand will be satisfied with falling unit costs. In such circumstances the demand for new capital instruments in the early stage of recovery will probably be small. It is also assumed that the loan-financed public works will not be met by new hoarding. Experience seems to show that the effectiveness of this policy in changing producers' anticipations depends a great deal on the political complexion of the Government. The Swedish Labour Administration did encounter temporary sabotage on the part of the commercial banks when it launched its public works policy in the spring of 1933 ; but the British National Government would have been free from this handicap.

The "cost" of public works is a much discussed topic. The die-hard critics who regard public investments as artificial rate the expense very high. On the other hand, enthusiasts for the policy argue that at the bottom of a slump they really cost the country nothing. The answer lies midway. Modern industrial states admit the necessity of providing relief for unemployed workers at a certain subsistence level. The cost of unemployment relief is borne as a fixed charge on the budgets of all income recipients. Since the absorption of unemployed into public works diminishes this burden of relief, the "cost" to the state must be less than the amount spent for the purpose.[1] Any calculation of social cost must also take into account the long-run effect on the physique and morale of workers who would otherwise remain idle.

The problem of the choice of works must be considered in the light of the economic structure of the country. If the export trade consists largely of capital goods, as in the case of Sweden, public works of a high labour intensity, in the sense of a large proportion of wages to total outlay, will not do much to alleviate unused capacity in the capital industries. The closed system analysis loses much of its point in these circumstances. Large expenditure on roads or relief payments, by stimulating the demand for consumers' goods, will give some benefit to the instrumental trades. But if the object is to give a direct fillip to the idle capital industries, the State's expenditure must imply a relatively large demand for investment goods. If this can only be done by increasing the demand for complementary raw materials from abroad, it will, *ceteris paribus*, curtail the international margin.

[1] Cf. Pigou, *Economics in Practice*, pp. 47–8.

We must now analyse the effects of a public works programme on the assumption of a narrow international margin.[1] For this purpose we need a fairly realistic model of an open system, consisting of two structures of production. One of them produces capital goods for export, and the other consumers' goods mainly for internal demand. The profits of the capital goods industries depend chiefly on foreign conditions of demand and the price policy of competitors. Some of their output can be sold on the home market in the event of an increase in demand derived from a higher level of internal consumption. But the same causes may be expected to raise the production costs of the export trades and weaken their competitive position abroad. Any primary change which increases production, real income, and prices in the industries relying on the home market may be expected, other things being equal, to diminish the volume of exports. On the other hand, it will tend to bring about an increase in imports owing to higher consumption and a demand for foreign raw materials and certain consumers' goods. There will be an adverse influence on the physical balance of trade. The effect on capital movements is difficult to decide. If it is a small country with a sound long-period budgetary system,

[1] Cf. Myrdal, op. cit., part iv, chapters iv and v; and Ohlin, *Penningpolitik, offentliga arbeten, subventioner och tullar som medel mot arbetslöshet* (1934), chapter v.

there might be an inflow of capital. A large country, possessing a key position in the world's capital markets and running its budget on orthodox lines, might suffer from a flight of capital. It all depends on the various elements underlying the risk valuations of the owners of short-term capital. If the country is on an independent standard, and the public works programme causes an adverse balance, the authorities may, of course, allow the external value of the currency to depreciate. In practice there is a limit to this method of creating the necessary margin, in view of foreign retaliation and probable loss of confidence. As soon as this limit is reached, the country will be confronted with an absolute shortage of capital. Any further extension of public investment will then be a barren transfer of resources made at the expense of private enterprise.

The problem is, therefore, to finance the public works in such a way as to maximize the beneficial effect on business within the available margin. There is a case for financing some of the State investments through taxation which discourages consumption—assuming that it will not be offset by inroads into savings. More important is the desirability of combining with the public works programme a moderate reduction of wage rates in public and private industry.[1] The

[1] Cf. Myrdal, *Konjunktur och offentliga hushållning*, p. 42: *Åtgarder mot arbetslöshet* (*Unemployment Commission Report*), vol. ii (1935), p. 152 ff.

object of this is to damp down the increase in consumption which would otherwise take place. It must be emphasized that without the public works, such wage cutting measures would probably have a deflationary effect in these circumstances. But, as part of a general expansionist policy, they are necessary in view of the threat to the supply of capital due to the restricted international margin. Duties on certain classes of imports might also be useful in helping to maintain the international margin. Finally, it is possible to apply measures which tend to widen the margin, though not all of them would simultaneously have a favourable effect on internal conditions. All sorts of combinations of policies are conceivable. Given the situation of a particular country, it is desirable to choose the best combination of measures calculated to induce recovery. The State is in the unique position of being able to take over some of the risks which the private entrepreneurs are afraid to undertake; and thus, by altering the basis of their anticipations, it can set in motion an upward swing which will have a cumulative character. We are not here concerned with the important question as to when such an upward process begins to become "inflationary".

(5) Credit Policy

The emphasis in this chapter is not on the influence of the loan rate of interest. Cheap money by itself cannot stimulate new investment at this stage of the depression. Credit policy, however, has an important part to play. The success of any expansionist programme depends on co-operation between the Exchequer and the Central Bank. If credit conditions for private industry are stiffened during the launching of public works, the effect on business conditions might be depressing. Moreover, speculation in long-term bonds might prove embarrassing. When a large-scale public borrowing operation is expected, speculators might withhold their purchases of gilt-edged securities and perhaps sell out. This would drive up the long-term rate of interest. It is essential that the Central Bank should be prepared to pursue open market policy to prevent this development.

Sharp reductions in bank rate must be made to have an early effect on the long-term rate. This is not always easy. The conversion operation in England in 1932 was a good example of the enormous benefit which follows State action to force down the long-term rate. But there may still be hindrances which prevent the low rate from being effective for borrowers. It was only at an advanced stage in the building boom in England that the rate of interest fell even to 4 per cent. The outburst of activity was to some extent due to factors on the demand side, e.g. the increase in the number of marriages following on the postponement which was a feature of the slump years 1930–2. In a country like Sweden where the savings banks are an important part of the banking system, it was often difficult to get their rates of interest into line with the bank rate.

Great advantages may follow from an official declaration regarding the policy to be pursued by the Central Bank.[1] This tends to create confidence and diminishes the risks which beset people's calculations in times of uncertainty. There can be no doubt that the official statement in Sweden in 1931 that the policy of the Riksbank would be " to maintain the internal purchasing power of the krona " had this effect. It is hardly necessary to add that the bank must be equipped with a sufficient stock of foreign exchange and must be prepared to use it in order to prevent undue fluctuations in the rate of exchange. A bearish tendency in foreign exchange speculation would have serious consequences, particularly if the authorities were anxious to preserve an already restricted international margin. The task of the Central Bank would be rendered extremely difficult if it could not find means of controlling such speculation. It should organize a forward market in foreign exchange, so that it may influence speculators' anticipations in the proper direction.

[1] See Ohlin, op. cit., p. 89.

Mere reliance on bank rate policy whether during a boom or a depression is not sufficient. We have already shown its weaknesses during the War-time inflation. It is often necessary in times of crisis to resort to credit discrimination, as, for example, the Riksbank did in 1931–2 when it advised the commercial banks to exercise restraint in granting credits to importers. Changes in policy adopted towards the "fringe of unsatisfied borrowers" could be a useful subsidiary to a general expansionist policy.

Experience of recovery measures in recent years has demonstrated the difficulty of inducing business improvement by merely pumping more money into circulation. A credit expansion presupposes an increase in investment; and the increase in investment is bound up with credit expansion. This vicious circle can only be broken, as we have emphasized, if the State takes upon itself the risks and starts an upward process by means of a policy of public investment.

(6) Wages Policy

The theoretical propositions outlined in Chapter III emphasized the fact that the upward and downward swings are cumulative and that a reversal of any existing tendency comes about by way of individuals' anticipations. A policy based on the diagnosis that the crisis is a symptom of a scarcity of capital may well lead to an accentuation of the slump. The condition for a sound revival is not that all the sins committed in the previous boom should first be painfully expiated, though a certain amount of liquidation is inevitable and necessary. The time is ripe for a revival of investment as soon as costs bear a favourable relation to expected future receipts. But the achievement of this new basis does not necessarily come most quickly and surely by adjustments on the cost side alone. This may be illustrated by touching upon the question of wages policy. A valuable study of this subject has been made by Dr. Alf Johansson, one of the younger Swedish economists.[1]

A change in wages has two aspects : it has an effect on producers' costs and on the volume of consumers' demand. Let us suppose that in a closed system producers of capital goods increase their wage disbursements by employing more labour at the same rates, on the expectation of a rise in the demand for their products. The addition to their wages bill, assuming no change in saving, will represent a corresponding rise in the demand for final commodities. If the consumption goods industries increase their demand for capital goods, the effect will be communicated from

[1] See Alf Johansson, *Löneutvecklingen och arbetslösheten* (Supplement to the *Unemployment Commission Report*, 1934).

stage to stage and the anticipations of the capital goods producers will be fulfilled. It is, thus, necessary that the additional wage payments should appear as demand for consumption goods and that the improvement in the last stage of production should be reflected back to the capital goods producers. It is also assumed that the latter allow stocks to accumulate in expectation of larger sales. Assuming many employers raise wages, it is all the more probable that their anticipations will be realized. If production were wholly integrated in the hands of a supreme authority this process would be more certain. Similarly, if we abstract from the effect on the relative demand for labour, a rise in wage rates in the capital goods industries without an equivalent fall in the quantity of labour employed can only prove justified if the new consumers' demand is transmitted back to those producers.[1]

If production is not integrated and the repercussions are not communicated from stage to stage, losses will be made and production will contract. When a boom has gathered strength and entrepreneurs in the constructional trades are optimistic, a rise in wages will not be an effective deterrent to expansion. The demand for labour in the short-run will be inelastic. Employers will not dismiss workers, but will carry larger stocks in anticipation of

[1] See *Åtgärder mot arbetslöshet* (1935), pp. 50–1.

a stronger derived demand for their products. This is equivalent to an excess of investment over saving, a factor which will tend to intensify the boom. If we confine ourselves to a closed system and ignore the possibility of widespread rationalization induced by the increase in wages, the effects seem to depend on the character of producers' expectations and the rapidity with which the derived demand for investment goods makes itself felt. A general cut in wages in the middle of a slump can be expected to aggravate the downward movement. But as soon as sufficient liquidations have been experienced and capital values are sensitive to recovery, a lowering of wage rates can be very beneficial. From the point of view of the volume of employment, this argument is reinforced by the consideration that, with reduced wages, entrepreneurs are less likely to choose investment plans which are labour-saving. An advance in wages as soon as the bottom of the slump has been passed is injurious, for it will add to costs at a time when producers are only beginning to feel slightly optimistic. As we have previously shown, a reduction in wages will have maximum effect at this stage only if it is accompanied by a programme of public investment.

The consequences of an adjustment in wages in an open system are more complicated. We may here revert to the example of a country on a paper standard with a relatively large export trade in capital goods, and assume that the demand for these products diminishes. Equilibrium can be achieved in three ways: wages can be reduced in the export trades without a falling off in employment; wages can remain stable with a corresponding volume of unemployment; the external value of the currency can be allowed to fall. Given a cut in wages, the same amount of goods as before may be sold abroad, but at lower prices. There need be no unemployment, but the total volume of income disbursed in the export trades will be lower. If the country's demand for imports is maintained, the bank will be obliged to stiffen credit conditions in order to protect the value of the currency. This will lead to a contraction of purchasing power in home industries, imports will decline and equilibrium can be restored. Unemployment cannot be avoided unless wages are cut in industries other than those directly affected by the fall in foreign demand. If the adjustment takes this form, the number in work will be unchanged, and their real income will not diminish more than is necessitated by the reduction in the volume of imports.[1]

Let us now drop the assumption of flexible wage rates. A smaller physical volume of exports will now be sold at the old prices, with

[1] Ibid., p. 72.

the result that some of the workers become unemployed. If the demand for imports is maintained the bank will restrict credit. The volume of output in the home market industries must decline, because bank credit is curtailed, wage costs are stable and income in the export trades has fallen. The price level will not be lowered as much as in the previous case. The contraction in consumers' income in both instances might be the same, but, where wages are rigid and the adjustment takes the form of unemployment, the diminution in the average real income of the workers will be greater. The disadvantage of rigidity is also apparent when we consider the possible effects on capital movements. Foreign creditors will be faced with two prospects: the rate of interest will have risen, and the fall in output and the rise in unemployment will have damaged business men's anticipations. It is probable that the creditors will attach more importance to the latter than to the former, and they may be prompted to terminate the granting of credits. If this leads to a net outflow of capital, the country's position will be further worsened.

The "costs" of overcoming wage rigidity are on the same footing as the "costs" of defeating business men's propensity to hoard. If the investing world is obsessed with the risk element, recovery will not come as a result of purely monetary measures. There are strong reasons for believing that carefully planned public investment in a depression diminishes risks and arrests the landslide towards liquid assets. The trade unions' resistance to a lowering of wage rates may, by precipitating disastrous stoppages, destroy the effect of other measures designed to create confidence. The country may, therefore, consider the third possibility, namely currency depreciation. If wages are a relatively small proportion of prime costs in the export industries affected by the decline in demand, there will be a decided pull in this direction. Supposing wages costs are 20 per cent of the value of the product and the latter falls by 10 per cent, then it will need a wage cut of 50 per cent if the industry is to continue to market the same output and unemployment is to avoided.[1]

It may be argued that rates of pay must also be lowered in trades producing instrumental goods sold to the export industries, so that other costs may fall. Such an adjustment would have the advantages which have already been pointed out. The disadvantages of altering the value of the currency must be borne in mind. It is likely to lead to retaliation from other countries, and a general resort to this easy remedy can only be ruinous. Moreover, the export trades will not get the full

[1] A Swedish committee of inquiry gave these figures as representative of Swedish industry. See *Åtgärder mot arbetslöshet*, p. 74.

benefit of the relief if they use auxiliary products purchased abroad.

Finally, a country may choose to ease its position by using the tariff instrument. There are important theoretical objections to this policy. If it is to be acceptable as a means of maintaining the international margin, it must be proved that less detrimental methods are not available, But, assuming unemployment of labour and capital, we may note the effects of a duty on a commodity for which the elasticity of demand is greater than the unity. After the tax is put on, the total value of the imported commodity, including the proceeds of the duty, will fall. A proportion of the consumers' outlay will have been released for the purchase of other goods. If this demand is directed towards substitutes produced at home and if there is unemployment in those industries, there will be an increase in output and an absorption of labour leading to a rise in incomes. If there is already full employment in these domestic trades, the new demand will increase incomes and indirectly stimulate activity elsewhere. Some assumption must be made about the use which the State makes of the proceeds of the duty. The receipts may be utilized to purchase home produced commodities. It is conceivable that the revival in demand for home products, by making entrepreneurs more confident, may result in additional borrowings from the banks. Assuming part of the new income is used to purchase other imported goods, the total value of the country's imports may be the same as it was before the duty was imposed. The net effect of the duty will have been to redistribute income and transfer demand from one group of foreign goods to others. There is, therefore, no necessity in this case for exports to fall off. On the assumption of full employment, costs would rise in the export trades partly because the home industries would compete for their factors of production and partly because some of the new income in domestic trades would be used to purchase the products of the export industries.[1] But, given unemployment, the importance of these reactions would be insignificant. Even in this favourable case, however, the evil effects of retaliatory tariffs in foreign countries would more than offset the benefits.

(7) The Advantages and Disadvantages of a Small Country

The consequences of measures designed to induce business revival vary according to whether the country is large or small and whether its foreign trade contributes an important share of its national income. Other things being equal, if a country is very small

[1] *Åtgärder mot arbetslöshet*, p. 84.

the foreign demand for its products is likely to be highly elastic. There are numerous alternative sources of supply of similar commodities and, therefore, a given change in price is likely to involve a more than proportionate movement in demand. It would appear that this puts a small country at a disadvantage. But the fact of size may be more than counterbalanced by the imperfection of the market. This may take the form of consumers' inertia, or the attachment of foreign buyers to the brand of goods produced in the particular country.

There is reason to believe that this has been true of Sweden. Technical developments in the large markets in the post-War period have created a rising demand for the commodities in which Sweden specializes. This is not only of quantitative importance, but it has been accompanied by the fact that the special quality of Swedish goods has made the demand less elastic than would be inferred from the smallness of Sweden relatively to the markets. It is a feature of Sweden's foreign trade that the five leading export products, namely, pulp, machines, timber, iron ore, and paper, constitute no less than 60 per cent of the total value of exports, and they are sold for the most part in Great Britain, the United States, Germany, and France. Her imports, on the other hand, are much more varied and are distributed fairly evenly over a large number of countries. It would have been easy for Sweden to pile on import duties without much fear of retaliation ; but it is to her credit that she has resorted less than most countries to the tariff weapon during the world depression.

The chief advantage of a small country is that it can pursue an expansionist policy within its international margin without bringing into play serious reactions from abroad. Any detrimental effect which the policy may have on foreign countries will be so widely diffused that the repercussions can be safely ignored. This is not true of a large country, especially if it has a considerable foreign trade. Every measure applied will produce reactions from abroad, and some of them may immediately defeat the end in view. It is hazardous to apply to England or the United States all the measures appropriate to Sweden. Much more depends on the large country's choice of measures. If it adopts tariffs or depreciates its currency drastically, the rest of the world may be forced to defend itself by resorting to similar weapons, and the result will be restriction all round. On the other hand, if a substantial increase in investment can be secured quickly, the stimulus of higher prices and increased trade will be communicated to other countries. The reactions in this case will be mutually beneficial.

Much depends too, on the structure of the

small country's economic system. If it devotes a good proportion of its resources to producing capital goods for export, the demand for which is elastic, it may well suffer violent fluctuations. Our analysis of War-time inflation in Sweden proved that extraordinary circumstances are possible in which the external demand financed on credit can cause a feverish boom. An inflation in a large system, by increasing the demand for raw materials and instrumental goods, can have a very disturbing effect on the direction of investment in the exporting country. If the price and income structure is rigid and the demand for its exports is elastic, a series of induced booms will tend to drive the country towards self-sufficiency. Too much mobility will be demanded of the system. It will seek to make itself less susceptible to outside forces, at the price of lowering productivity. It will be prepared to sacrifice some of its opulence in exchange for more stability.

During the post-War decade Sweden was becoming more sensitive owing to her closer connection with the world's short-term capital markets. The transactions carried out by Ivar Kreuger were a clear indication of Sweden's new status as a financial centre. Experience in recent years has shown what disturbing consequences can arise from the migration of short-term balances. The reputation of England and Sweden for political stability makes them attractive centres for such assets. When a small country harbours a relatively large volume of short-term capital, a dangerous situation can ensue ; the real facts are masked and there is a heightened possibility of the monetary authorities being misled. One of the chief difficulties of a reconstituted international standard will be to reconcile the rigidity of income structures with the readjustments necessary if international equilibrium is to be maintained.

Chapter V

EXPANSION AND DEPRESSION IN SWEDEN, 1924–1932

As an introduction to the analysis of the measures taken to cope with the recent depression in Sweden, it is proposed in this chapter to comment briefly on some aspects of her economic development in the 'twenties. The great slump of the early 'thirties was no respecter of countries: the just as well as the unjust were dragged in its train. But the origin of the weakness was not the same in every country.

It is essential to distinguished between what have been called "autonomous" and "induced" booms. When an inflationary expansion takes place within one large member of an international group, the stimulus is communicated to other members through the rise in certain groups of prices. The nature of the adjustment necessitated by a crisis must vary to some extent according to whether the previous boom has been autonomous or induced. We shall proceed to examine Swedish experience in this light.

(1) Production, Prices, and Productivity

Sweden led the way in 1924 by returning to the gold standard at pre-War parity. Five years of steady expansion followed.

In the period 1924–9 the physical volume of production expanded from 106 to 147 (1915 = 100), whereas the wholesale price level fell from 162 to 140 (1913 = 100). There was nothing unique about this, for the course of the wholesale level was similar in England and the United States.

Wholesale Price Level (1913 = 100)

	1920.	*1921.*	*1922.*	*1923.*	*1924.*	*1925.*	*1926.*	*1927.*	*1928.*	*1929.*
Sweden [1] .	359	222	173	163	162	161	149	146	148	140
England [2] .	307	197	159	159	166	159	148	141	140	137
U.S.A.[3] . .	221	140	138	144	140	148	143	137	140	138

Let us now examine production and productivity in more detail. Physical output in production goods industries rose from 103 in 1924 to 150 in 1929, while in consumption goods industries the advance was smaller, namely from 109 to 143. The output per man-hour increased in the former group from 128 to 150 and in the latter from 119 to 136. There appears to have been more rationalization in the former group. Further evidence may be obtained from statistics of the course of wages, value of the product per man-hour, and the price of the product in different branches of industry.

[1] Kommerskollegium index.
[2] Board of Trade's general index.
[3] Bureau of Labor statistics.

1929 [1] (1924–6 = 100)

Group.	*Money wages.*	*Value of product per man-hour.*	*Price of product.*
Iron Ore and Metal	107·8	111·0	96·2
Mining and Quarrying	95·1	103·0	92·8
Wood	107·1	102·3	93·9
Paper	108·1	107·3	90·8
Chemicals	103·6	106·6	91·0
Foodstuffs	106·2	101·7	88·7
Textiles and Clothing	100·0	95·2	91·5
Leather, Hair, and Rubber	100·9	96·8	92·4
All Groups	106·8	103·4	91·8

The increases in value of product per man-hour between 1924–6 and 1929 were most prominent in the iron ore, metal, paper, chemical, mining, quarrying and wood industries, whereas there was actually a decline in the textiles, clothing, leather, hair and rubber trades. Another striking fact is that the imports of capital goods for industrial purposes into Sweden rose by 87 per cent in the period 1924–9, while the volume of production increased by 39 per cent. The table on p. 160 shows the position for industry as a whole.[2]

The engineering industry, in particular, exhibits a clear parallelism between the upward movement of wages, the import of capital

[1] Based on Appendix E (by E. Dahlgren) to vol. i of the *Unemployment Commission Report* (1931) (*Arbetslöshetens omfattning, karaktär och orsaker.*)

[2] See Dag Hammarskjöld, *Konjunkturspridningen* (*Statens offentliga utredningar, 1933*, 29), p. 155.

goods, and physical productivity. Corroborative proof is available in Professor Gustav Åkerman's detailed studies of industrial rationalization,[1] that the main incentive to mechanization in this industry was the high wage rate. In the

Industry as a Whole.	*1922.*	*1923.*	*1924.*	*1925.*	*1926.*	*1927.*	*1928.*	*1929.*
Imports of capital goods (million kronor) . .	32·4	33·9	37·3	38·3	42·4	47·1	56·8	69·6
Money wages (1922 = 100) . . .	100·0	95·0	97·0	100·0	102·0	103·0	104·0	106·0
Output per man-hour (1922 = 100) .	100·0	99·0	101·0	102·0	106·0	107·0	110·0	115·0
Engineering.	*1922.*	*1923.*	*1924.*	*1925.*	*1926.*	*1927.*	*1928.*	*1929.*
Imports of capital goods (million kronor) . .	2·9	2·3	3·2	3·8	4·3	4·7	6·4	9·9
Nominal wages (1922 = 100) . .	100	93	96	97	99	100	101	102
Output per man-hour (1922 = 100) .	100	98	98	99	104	107	114	118

textile industry the price of the product fell by about 8·5 per cent between 1924–6 and 1929 while wages remained more or less constant. The effect on relative wages cost may be seen in the following computation [2] :—

Relative Labour Cost in the Textile Industry (1922 = 100)

1922.	*1923.*	*1924.*	*1925.*	*1926.*	*1927.*	*1928.*	*1929.*
100	104	108	109	110	114	113	113

The substantial drop in the price of textile products made it impossible to avoid a fall in the value of the product per man-hour in spite of mechanization.

These figures suggest that over a large part of the Swedish economy in the period 1924–9

[1] G. Åkerman, *Om den industriella rationaliseringen och dess verkningar* (*Statens offentliga utredningar*, *1931*, 42), pp. 22–7.

[2] See D. Hammarskjöld, op. cit., p. 156.

the rigidity of wages was a major cause of the progress of rationalization, which led to abnormal imports of capital goods for mechanization purposes. According to the following indices [1] the quantity of money seems to have been fairly stable during the years 1926–1930.

	Cheque deposits.	*Deposits subject to notice.*	*Unused overdrafts.*	*Total.*
		(million kronor).		
1926 (January)	421	329	249	999
1927 „	422	283	271	976
1928 „	430	252	295	977
1929 „	418	266	287	971
1930 „	416	293	273	982

There was a relative contraction in deposits subject to notice and a relative rise in unused overdrafts ; but the general trend of the volume of money, not allowing for the velocity of circulation, remained more or less constant.

(2) Wages

The course of wages in Sweden since the War shows a tendency for wide divergences to appear between the remuneration of different groups of work-people. The cleavage between agriculture (including forestry) and industry is brought out by the following table.

Daily Wage Rates in Industry, Agriculture, and Forestry [2]

	1913.	*1920.*	*1921.*	*1922.*	*1923.*	*1924.*	*1925.*	*1926.*	*1927.*	*1928.*	*1929.*
Agriculture . .	100	316	227	170	160	161	160	159	159	159	159
Forestry . .	100	323	146	158	168	159	162	158	159	155	162
Industry, Building, etc. . . .	100	309	305	223	213	214	220	223	223	225	232

[1] See D. Hammarskjöld, *Konjunkturspridningen*, p. 138.

[2] *Unemployment Commission Report*, vol. i (1931), p. 163.

The adjustment in wages in the immediate post-War slump was much more rapid in agriculture and forestry than in industry. Wages in forestry fell from 323 to 146 in 1920–1, whereas in industry they hardly moved at all. From 1922 onwards a constant disparity has been maintained. When we turn to industry we observe further differences. If 1930 is compared with 1913, we get the following increases in hourly earnings [1]: building (248 per cent), transport (240 per cent), and food products (202 per cent). On the other hand, the smallest increases are found in mineral and quarrying (151 per cent), wood products (154 per cent), and textile and clothing (154 per cent). Compared with 1913 the hourly earnings of skilled workers in the engineering industry in 1928 went up by 134·8 per cent, while the increase for unskilled was 152·1 per cent. In the second half of 1931 the general cost of living was 58 per cent above 1914—an average concealing a wide dispersion. It is remarkable that rents went up by no less than 106 per cent compared with only 28 per cent for foodstuffs.[2] There is, incidentally, an important connection between the uninterrupted rise in house rents since

[1] Bagge, Lundberg, and Svennilson, *Wages in Sweden, 1860–1930*, vol. i, p. 253.

[2] G. Myrdal, *The Cost of Living in Sweden, 1830–1930*, Mr. Sven Bouvin's Appendix, p. 171.

1923, the advance in builders' wages, and the strength of the building trade union.

It is important to find out to what extent the boom of 1927–9 distorted the Swedish structure of production and the part played by the elements of immobility to which we have drawn attention. We shall examine the data relating to production goods and consumption goods industries.[1] It is first necessary to observe the trend of the total labour supply in industry. Throughout the 'twenties there was a migration of a fluctuating character away from agriculture ; the net loss of population in agricultural communes expressed as an annual percentage of their population was as follows [2] :—

1923.	1924.	1925.	1926.	1927.	1928.	1929.
−0·65	−0·80	−0·59	−0·58	−0·45	−0·66	−0·93

But the migrants were by no means all absorbed in industry proper. The annual

[1] The *Industriförbund* publishes indices relating to production goods and consumption goods industries as well as home market and export industries. They appear with the other official statistics in *Kommersiella Meddelanden*, the monthly organ of the Swedish Board of Trade. The industries which are included in the capital group are mining, iron, metal, engineering (home and export), sawmilling, paper, pulp, quarrying and chemical industries. The consumption group comprises paper, textiles, leather, household goods (home and export), food, and entertainment. This is the broad division ; each industry is divided up into sections and these are allocated to the one group or the other. A detailed account of the statistical basis of these indices is to be found in Johan Åkerman, *Industriförbundets produktionsindex, motiv och principer* (*Sveriges Industriförbund*, 1932).

[2] *Unemployment Commission Report*, vol. i, p. 324.

percentage variations in the labour force within industry were not very considerable.

PERCENTAGE CHANGES IN LABOUR EMPLOYED [1]

	1913–20.	1920–1.	1921–2.	1922–3.	1923–4.
Industry	+15·7	−21·3	−0·7	+ 9·8	+6·0
Production goods	—	−27·0	−5·3	+15·6	+6·1
Consumption goods	—	−13·5	+4·8	+ 3·8	+6·0

	1924–5.	1925–6.	1926–7.	1927–8.	1928–9.
Industry	+3·2	+3·8	+0·8	+6·9	+3·4
Production goods	+4·5	+3·4	+1·8	+7·1	+4·3
Consumption goods	+1·6	+4·3	−0·3	+6·9	+2·1

One would have expected the changes in the number employed in production goods industries relatively to consumption goods industries to have been more pronounced. A more accurate picture may be obtained by expressing the proportion of each group to industry as a whole as a percentage of 1915.[2]

(1915 = 100)	1920.	1921.	1922.	1923.	1924.	1925.	1926.	1927.	1928.	1929.
Relation between number employed in production goods industries and in industry as a whole	101	94	90	94	94	95	95	96	96	97
Consumption goods industries ratio	99	108	114	108	108	106	107	106	106	104

During the years 1922–5, when a recovery was made from the severe post-War slump, there was a marked relative rise in employment in production goods industries and a relative fall in consumption goods industries. But between 1925 and 1928 the two series hardly diverge. It is only in 1929 that a mild symptom of a redistribution of labour typical of a boom becomes discernible. That there was a con-

[1] *Unemployment Commission Report*, vol. i, p. 464.
[2] Ibid.

siderable expansion in the production of capital goods relatively to consumption goods is brought out very clearly by the following figures [1] :—

(1915 = 100)	1920.	1921.	1922.	1923.	1924.
Output of capital goods / Total production	100	86	88	91	97
Output of consumption goods / Total production	100	115	112	110	103

(1915 = 100)	1925.	1926.	1927.	1928.	1929.
Output of capital goods / Total production	98	97	99	99	102
Output of consumption goods / Total production	102	103	101	101	97

Between the years 1926 and 1929, the index of the relative production of capital goods moved up from 97 to 102, whereas that for the production of consumption goods declined correspondingly. There was a real change in the structure of production as far as the character of output was concerned ; but it was not accompanied by anything like a corresponding movement of labour.

How far was this due to the splitting up of the general labour market into rigid small markets as a consequence of the monopolistic practices of trade unions ? To what extent was it the result of rationalization reducing the demand for labour in capital-producing industries ? It is impossible to give satisfactory

[1] Ibid., p. 465.

answers to these questions. But we can learn something from the relative movements of wages. In the following table the hourly wage rates in capital goods and consumption goods industries are calculated as percentages of the average wage level in industry as a whole.

WAGES PER HOUR AS PER CENT OF AVERAGE WAGE LEVEL IN INDUSTRY [1]

	1920.	1921.	1922.	1923.	1924.	1925.	1926.	1927.	1928.	1929
Production goods industries . . .	99	99	95	97	98	99	99	99	99	100
Consumption goods industries . . .	101	101	108	104	103	104	103	101	101	99

The Unemployment Commission interprets these figures as showing that the relative course of wages in the two groups of industries was fairly typical of an upward swing in the trade cycle. And yet throughout the boom period there was a volume of unemployment considerably above the Swedish average for pre-War years. The percentages of trade union members registered as unemployed were as follows :—

AVERAGE PERCENTAGE OF TRADE UNION MEMBERS UNEMPLOYED [2]

	1920.	1921.	1922.	1923.	1924.	1925.	1926.	1927.	1928.	1929.
Production goods industries . . .	6·5	34·1	28·0	15·3	12·1	12·1	14·1	14·0	11·5	11·3
Consumption goods industries . . .	4·1	22·5	19·0	10·1	7·0	8·0	9·0	8·9	8·4	8·3

(3) THE IMMOBILITY OF LABOUR

Sweden probably possesses as strong a trade union movement as any country in the world. Though about 10 per cent of the workers

[1] Ibid., p. 465. [2] Ibid., p. 448.

included in collective agreements are not in the trade unions, and 13 per cent of those within the unions are not covered by agreements, no less than 75 per cent of the workers in industry and transport are organized. After falling from 403,000 to 361,000 in the slump of 1920–2, the membership of trade unions rose to 550,000 by 1929.[1] Both armies are well organized for industrial warfare. There are over 2,000 employers' associations which have sought to make themselves something more potent than mere loose and formal alliances. Among their most effective weapons are the "black lists" and the labour registers which include full details of workers taken on and dismissed. Information from these registers is circulated among members of employers' associations, particularly in the transport, forestry, and iron industries, one of the objects being to prevent competition among employers when labour is scarce. The black lists are used to prevent the employment of workers involved in a trade dispute. Swedish employers, in the face of the strong encroachment of powerful, nationally-organized trade unions, have fought a long battle to maintain their full sovereignty over "hiring and firing". The unions have pressed the seniority rule and have insisted in having their say in the selection of workers. In some cases a provision that the

[1] Ibid., p. 384.

last to be signed on are to be the first to be dismissed has been inserted in the agreements.

Nothing is stronger evidence of the power of Swedish trade unions than the control they exercise over the movements of their members. It would be inaccurate to regard this as wholly detrimental to mobility. Wholesale denunciation of union practices as causes of rigidity overlooks the fact that increased knowledge of industrial conditions in various parts of the country diminishes costs of movement. But it must be admitted that union policy has tended to split up the general labour market into rigid compartments, and whereas their placing functions may increase mobility within each craft, they have diminished it as between different trades. A powerful method of controlling the labour supply in a trade is to insist on trade union membership as a necessary qualification for employment and then to refuse applications to join the union. Though the Central Association of Trade Unions (*Landsorganisationen*) has forcibly condemned this policy of exclusion, it is known to be practised particularly in the building and foodstuffs industries. The union does all it can to make unnecessary a rush of workers to the factory gates when the employer is in need of more hands. The migrating workers register themselves at the local trade union office and it is by arrangement with the union officials that the employer gets his extra labour. If he tries to ignore the union and select his workers as he likes, he may find his factory boycotted. This use of the register by the unions is most common in the typography, bakery, butchery, and metal trades, and similar practices are not unknown among workers in iron foundries, highway and water works, and building. The Unemployment Commission also noted that the frequent insistence of unions on equal pay for men and women and the lowering of the age at which a man receives the full adult wage (noticeable in iron, mechanical engineering, saw-milling, pulp, and match-making industries) have in certain directions curtailed employment for women and young men between the ages of 18 and 21. A characteristic of post-War years has been the increasing spread of the national agreement which has tended towards an equalization of individual earnings between different districts. On the other hand the average duration of collective agreements is shorter than before the War, as the following interesting table shows.

AVERAGE DURATION OF COLLECTIVE AGREEMENTS [1] (PERCENTAGES OF TOTAL).

Year.	*1 year and under.*	*Over 1 and under 2 years.*	*Over 2 and under 3 years.*	*Over 3.*	*Unclassified.*
1908 .	32·3	37·6	22·3	2·6	5·2
1920 .	81·6	16·5	0·2	—	1·7
1922 .	99·0	0·8	—	—	0·2
1929 .	52·2	41·0	4·1	0·1	2·6

[1] Ibid., p. 383.

Before the War one-quarter of the agreements were valid for periods of over two years; the uncertainties of post-War years have led to the virtual disappearance of such agreements.

Sweden has no compulsory State system of unemployment insurance. Since 1884 the trade unions have distributed out of work pay to their members, the average amount of which was 13·54 kronor weekly per member in 1926 compared with 3·54 kronor in 1913.[1] Unemployment relief is organized in the form of special public works (*reservarbeten*) administered chiefly by the municipalities, the wage-rate averaging about 15 per cent below trade union rates. It is estimated that one half of the workless in Sweden receive no assistance; and there is a growing demand that the country should complete its system of social services by adopting the principle of compulsory State insurance. Swedish experience demonstrates the hollowness of the claim that, if trade unions are saddled with the duty of looking after their own unemployed members, the labour market will tend to approximate to the atomistic ideal of the pure theorist. The relief schemes of municipalities are inevitably tainted with parish-pump protectionism; and in any case the assistance they provide is inadequate. A combination of such schemes with voluntary trade union insurance which

[1] See C. J. Ratzlaff, *The Scandinavian Unemployment Relief Program* (1934), chapters iv, vii, and viii.

does nothing to reduce inflexibility is a poor substitute for a national system of insurance on the British model.

The broad effect of the above-mentioned developments has been to weaken the responsiveness of the supply price of labour to changed conditions and to enhance the significance of non-competing groups in the general labour market.[1] A summary table will serve to illustrate this.[2]

THE COURSE OF RELATIVE LABOUR COST AND PHYSICAL PRODUCTIVITY

	1920.	*1924.*	*1925.*	*1926.*	*1927.*	*1928.*	*1929.*
Workers per unit of product (1915 = 100)	119	95	95	91	89	90	82
Product per man-hour (1915 = 100)	102	125	126	132	133	136	143
Relative Labour Cost per hour:							
(*a*) Real Wage (1913 = 100)	135	138	140	146	148	150	155
(*b*) Nominal Hour-wage / Raw Material price index (1913=100)	98	160	160	177	183	178	194
(*c*) Nominal Hour-wage / Price of Industrial Products (1913 = 100)	108	141	146	165	159	162	171

Relative labour cost as expressed by the relation between wages per man-hour and the price of industrial products increased by 71 per cent between 1913 and 1929; physical productivity as measured by the output per man-hour rose by 43 per cent between 1915 and 1929. Especially striking is the fact that the most rapid advances of relative labour cost (1925–6 and 1928–9) coincided with the greatest increases in physical productivity. The statistics

[1] See Professor Bagge's authoritative theoretical study, *Orsaker till arbetslöshet,* contributed as a supplement to the Unemployment Commission Report (1931).

[2] *Unemployment Commission Report,* vol. i, p. 446.

tend to emphasize the suggestion already made that much of the rationalization was induced by high wages; and we also know that it took place to a considerable extent in capital producing industries. Simultaneously with the sharp rise in the supply price of labour there was an increase in the population in the age-group 16–65 of 400,000 in the decade 1921–1930 compared with corresponding increases of 275,000 in 1901–1910 and 374,000 in 1911–1920. On the other hand, the national income, allowing for the change in the value of money, was 30 per cent higher in 1927 than in 1913; this represented a rise of 20 per cent per head of the population. There is strong reason for thinking that the volume of savings grew at least in the same proportion. Yet this was not sufficient to counterbalance the factors making for unemployment even at the height of the boom. The Unemployment Commission argued that both rigidity in the labour market and rationalization greatly reduced the amount of redistribution of labour which the boom of 1926–9 would otherwise have occasioned. Moreover, the low degree of mobility between agriculture and industry proper may have helped to prevent an unhealthy concentration of labour in industries which have rigid wage rates and are particularly susceptible to boom conditions.[1] This argument is not convincing.

[1] Ibid., p. 499. See also Prof. G. Bagge, "Wages and Unemployment in Sweden 1920–30," *Essays in Honour of G. Cassel*, p. 703.

It rests on the false assumption that immobility of labour does not aggravate cyclical fluctuation. Carried to its logical conclusion this would mean that, if the labour market were completely rigid, the disproportions induced by an inflation would be minimized. But this cannot be true. If the price mechanism, as regards wages, is paralysed by immobility, the probability that producers' anticipations will be falsified is greatly increased. The structure of prices is distorted and capital and labour are uneconomically distributed. The result is lower productivity and higher unemployment. The argument also seems to assume that it is " desirable " that a certain proportion of the population should be employed in a particular branch of production—agriculture. But this idea rests on non-economic motives and is irrelevant to an economic discussion. Even in the case of an inflation induced by temporary outside forces, it is wrong to think that artificial hindrances to movement guarantee the maintenance of some " correct " distribution of labour.

(4) The Course of Foreign Trade

Sweden's internal situation up to 1929 can be seen in its true significance only in the light of the development of her foreign trade. The total value of imports and exports per capita increased from 446 kronor in 1924 to 588 kronor in 1929. In comparison with the five years 1909–1913, allowance being made for the change in the value of money, the post-War period exhibited an expansion of 38 per cent in exports, and 33 per cent in imports; and total foreign trade per capita rose by 20 per cent. If we classify together the industries whose exports increased faster than the volume of production in the period 1913–1928, we find that as a group they employ no less than 45 per cent of the industrial population. Sweden's economy is therefore very sensitive to changes in the outside world.

As soon as the adjustment to the post-War situation was complete the terms of trade became very favourable. This is shown by the following figures of import and export prices.

	1921.	*1923.*	*1925.*	*1927.*	*1929.*
Average price of exports (1913 = 100)	209	168	153	146	144
Average price of imports	170	148	139	126	126
Terms of trade	81	88	91	87	87

Important shifts took place in the direction of the export trade.

THE DIRECTION OF EXPORTS [1] (PER CENT)

Destination.	*1913.*	*1920.*	*1927.*	*1929.*
Germany	23	9	17	15
Great Britain and Ireland	29	36	28	25
U.S.A.	5	6	11	11
Denmark, Norway, Finland	17	16	14	15
Holland and Belgium	5	7	6	7
France	9	8	4	6
Brazil and Argentine	2	2	2	2
Spain and Italy	2	4	4	4
Other Countries	8	12	14	15
	100	100	100	100

[1] Based on *Unemployment Commission Report*, vol. i, p. 209.

Swedish exports are concentrated in a few markets; Germany, Great Britain, and the United States accounted for no less than half her trade in 1929; there has also been a steady expansion in sales to distant overseas countries. The boom years 1927–9, in contrast to 1920, revealed the strong pulls exerted by the United States, Germany, and distant countries, though Great Britain still remained the best customer. The total value of exports rose, as we have seen, from 1,261 million kronor in 1924 to 1,812 millions in 1929.

The central problem is whether this expansion in the export trade was a result of internal price relationships in Sweden or of external factors which were powerful enough to give an inflationary twist to the Swedish system. In so far as an answer may be got from statistics, we have no reason to believe that internal price relationships were at all important. A comparison of the course of export prices with hourly wages in export trades does not point to any explanation in the sphere of relative prices.[1]

	1925.	*1926.*	*1927.*	*1928.*	*1929.*
Relation between price index for export goods and the index for home produced goods (1913 relation = 100)	93·3	100·7	102·1	99·3	100·7
Hourly wages in export trades as percentage of hourly wages in industry generally	94·1	95·0	95·8	95·1	95·2

[1] See D. Hammarskjöld, *Konjunkturspridningen*, pp. 193–4.

Swedish exports are made up largely of capital goods. Therefore our previous analysis of the progress of production goods industries relatively to consumption goods industries is relevant. It is clear that in the years leading up to 1929 resources were being drawn more and more into industries producing for export—particularly engineering, wood pulp, and paper. Some idea of the distribution of capital accumulation over different parts of the system may be obtained from the following figures.[1]

	Consumption.	*Agriculture.*	*Industry.*	*Remaining Branches (Roads, Building, Transport, etc.).*
Percentage share in total growth of capital goods, 1925–29 .	51	9	16	24
Growth of capital goods in 1929 as percentage of 1924 . . .	127	121	168	159

The quantitative importance of the expansion of investment in industry comes out clearly. The fact that this was concentrated mainly on export trades is supported by the trend of stock exchange quotations.[2]

We must again emphasize that the movement of labour into the export industries was much less than that of capital resources (table, p. 177). These nine branches of industry developed very favourably under the influence of the export boom; but only three of them—mechanical engineering, paper, and paper board

[1] Ibid., p. 196. [2] Ibid., p. 193.

THE INCREASE IN EXPORT VALUES, VOLUME OF PRODUCTION, PRODUCTIVITY AND NUMBER OF WORKERS IN CERTAIN EXPORT INDUSTRIES [1] 1928

	Value of Exports, 1913 = 100.	*Volume of production,* 1915 = 100.	*Output per man-hour,* 1915 = 100.	*Number of Workers,* 1915 = 100.
Mechanical Engineering .	420	178	170	122
Metal manufacture . .	330	149	145	117
Paper, paper-board . .	304	166	166	145
Iron, steel manufacture .	290	137	138	117
Matches	286	95	164	67
Pulp	235	155	160	147
Mineral	219	64	170	72
Saw Milling	{211 / 152}	123	140	112
Iron, steel rails . .	108	87	134	85
Industry as a whole . .	—	130	136	117

and pulp—showed an increase in employment greater than the average for industry as a whole.

Two fundamental forces were at work in the period 1924–9 forcing an expansion in Swedish exports. First, the primary boom in the United States and Germany made itself felt in the form of a greatly increased demand for capital goods; secondly, a favourable secular shift in the demand for products in which Sweden specializes. The internal price structure was not so much a determinant of the increased production of investment goods, but was itself moulded by the external factors. It follows that a greater degree of monetary expansion within Sweden in those years would not necessarily have diminished the prosperity of the export trades. It is an instructive example of how, under an international gold standard, a gold inflation is communicated from the larger to the smaller members of the group. In such circumstances countries which have

[1] *Unemployment Commission Report,* vol. i, p. 222.

enjoyed the benefits of an induced boom by playing according to the rules of the game may well be excused for protesting loudly, on the day of reckoning, that they have not sinned.

Among the secular factors which favoured Sweden may be mentioned the enormous increase in the consumption of paper. In the United States the expansion between 1911–13 and 1927–9 was no less than 110 per cent. Moreover the Swedish engineering industry has a special technical superiority in the production of telephones, ball-bearings, separators, etc., the demand for which has shown much buoyancy.

(5) The Depression and the Break from Gold

In retrospect the year 1929 is known as the fatal turning-point which inaugurated the great international slump. But few people at the time dreamt that the reaction would be so catastrophic. The Swedish Finance Minister, in his review of economic prospects accompanying the budget estimates in January, 1929,[1] commented on the abnormal stock exchange boom in the United States; but, apart from this, he thought the economic situation there was sound and stable and would probably

[1] *Bilagor till 1929 års statsverksproposition*, 1929, pp. 2–5.

continue so. As far as the Swedish position was concerned he deplored the disastrous stoppages of work which had disorganized industry in 1928, and had resulted in a fall in iron ore exports to half the volume of 1927, a serious reduction in the revenues of railways and a substantial deficit in the commodity balance of trade. Given the blessings of industrial peace he saw nothing which was likely to darken the horizon. Even a year later, in January, 1930, the new Minister was not very disturbed by the trend of events. He seemed to regard the American stock market collapse as merely the bursting of a nasty blister. " It is the general expectation," he wrote, " that the recession in trade will be overcome relatively quickly." As for Sweden he based his estimates on a continuance of favourable conditions in the main export industries—iron-ore, engineering, and wood pulp. Unless prices took a swift turn downwards Sweden's sound position would not be affected. He concluded that " for the financial year 1930–1 there is no reason for anticipating that economic conditions will be less favourable than in 1929 ".[1]

By January, 1931, another change had been made at the Finance Ministry. The new minister pointed out that his predecessor's diagnosis had been too optimistic : the latter

[1] *Bilagor till 1930 års statsverksproposition*, p. 5.

half of 1930 had brought a serious set-back. Nevertheless the outlook was not dark. Sweden's banking system was free from all danger; the liquidity of industrial enterprises was satisfactory; and the business recession would be mild and short-lived compared with the experience of less fortunate countries.[1]

Nothing is easier, after the event, than to take cynical pleasure in exposing the short-sightedness of men in authority. A feeling of measured optimism was excusable in Sweden, for the country did not feel the depression in any real sense until late in 1930. Some indices of the economic situation in the first half of 1929, 1930, and 1931 give the following picture.[2]

	Total volume of production.	*Volume of production in export industry.*	*Number employed in industry.*	*Number employed in export trades.*	*Price level of manu-factured goods.*	*Price level of exports.*
1929 First half	109	116	103	104	144	144
1930 ,, ,,	108	119	105	105	127	138
1931 ,, ,,	89	90	99	94	113	123

The total volume of production in the first six months of 1930 was almost up to the level of the corresponding period of 1929, while the volume of output and the number employed in the export trades actually increased. It was the price barometer which gave reason for anxiety in 1930.

The fundamental causes of the crisis of 1931

[1] *Bilagor till 1931 års statsverksproposition*, p. 3.

[2] Based on *Industriförbundet* figures. See Johan Åkerman, *Industriförbundets produktionindex*, Appendix.

are to be traced to the maladjustments in Sweden's system induced by the expansion of 1924–9. The immediate occasion for the departure from the gold standard is, however, to be sought in the sphere of international movements of short-term capital. Sweden had returned to gold in April, 1924, at the pre-War parity. Her price and income structure had undergone such a colossal deflation in 1920–3 that it would have been quite easy for her to link herself to gold even a year sooner. There was no question of the krona being over-valued. In fact it is not inconceivable that pre-War parity in 1924 constituted an under-valuation. We have seen how in the subsequent six years relative wages costs rose steadily, while the terms of trade were substantially in Sweden's favour. It is estimated that in the period 1926–1930 Sweden exported capital to the extent of no less than 730 million kronor. She was free from the millstone which England placed round her neck by returning to gold at pre-War parity in 1925.[1]

The drastic fall in the world prices of the commodities which constitute a large part of Sweden's imports made the terms of trade even more favourable in the early phase of the depression. Between December, 1929, and August, 1931, there was a decline of 33 per cent

[1] Cf. Professor E. E. Heckscher, *Sveriges penningpolitik* (1931), p. 14.

in the average price of imports compared with 20 per cent for exports.[1] In 1930 a visible import surplus of 114 millions was accompanied by a favourable balance of 214 millions on invisible account, so that there remained 100 millions for investment abroad. But this was not the whole story, for during that year there was a net import of securities to the extent of 337 millions.[2] Capital exports of this magnitude were only made possible because of an inflow of short-term balances from other countries resulting from the confidence crisis. Foreign deposits in Swedish banks rose by 138 millions to 217 millions; and the foreign exchange holdings of the Riksbank and other banks reached the high level of 400 millions by the end of 1930. We are justified in concluding that short-term borrowing was accompanied to a certain extent by long-term foreign lending.

The deterioration in the trade balance became extremely serious in the first half of 1931. Compared with the first eight months of 1930 the value of imports in the same period of 1931 fell from 1,238 to 1,049 millions, and that of exports from 1,150 to 795 millions. Such a situation, under the gold standard, clearly called for a rise in the discount rate

[1] These and the subsequent statistics are based for the most part on Dr. Karin Kock's paper, "Hur Sverige tvingades att överge guldmyntfoten," published in Professor Myrdal's *Sveriges väg genom penningkrisen* (1931), pp. 141–160.

[2] See Dr. Karin Kock "Paper Currency and Monetary Policy in Sweden," *Cassel Essays*, p. 344.

and a forcing down of the internal cost level. But the Riksbank reduced its discount rate in February, 1931, and kept it at 3 per cent until July, when it was raised to 4 per cent. The grim realities were masked by a renewed inflow of short term capital in the early months of 1931. The deposits of foreign banks in Sweden rose to the figure of 343 million kronor by the end of May—an increase of 126 millions on the beginning of the year; and we must add to this the deposits of private persons. The figures of imports and exports of securities exactly offset each other; but this does not mean that there was no export of capital in the first half of 1931. In particular the disturbing part played by the Kreuger and Toll undertaking must be noted. This concern was no longer able to finance its foreign loan operations by means of credits on the international market; so it had to fall back on Swedish banks. Two loans were raised in February and May, 1931, and the proceeds used to acquire foreign exchange to the detriment of the country's stock of foreign balances.[1] The result was that a growing commodity import surplus together with an export of capital was being made temporarily feasible by a sudden flow of short-term balances into the country.

[1] See Karin Kock, "Hur Sverige tvingades att överge guldmyntfoten," loc. cit., p. 145.

This precarious apple cart was rudely upset by the international rush for liquidity following upon the collapse of the Creditanstalt and the establishment of the German Standstill Agreement. Since 1924 Swedish funds amounting to 708 million kronor had been invested in German loans and the Standstill Agreement covered 90 millions. Then came a considerable run on the Swedish banks and in the months June–August no less than 216 millions of the foreign balances were withdrawn. The commodity import surplus could now only be financed by an inroad into the foreign exchange reserve of the Riksbank which fell by 155 millions to 125 million kronor in June–August. There was strong pressure on the pound sterling and the krona moved with it in accordance with the Swedish policy of maintaining a stable rate on sterling in the interests of her foreign trade. According to Swedish commentators,[1] foreigners interpreted this tendency as proving that Sweden's internal situation was as precarious as that of England. The krona was suspected owing to the bad company it kept!

The Riksbank had been aware of the dangers, and at the beginning of 1931 had pressed upon the commercial banks the desirability of limiting their purchases of foreign securities.[2] On the 6th February it had reduced the bank rate from

[1] e.g. Dr. Karin Kock, op. cit., pp. 151–2.

[2] *Bankoutskottets memorial*, No. 1 (16th January, 1932), p. 5.

$3\frac{1}{2}$ to 3 per cent in an endeavour to stem the inflow of capital. When the tide turned and the foreign balances took flight, the bank's first measure was to raise the discount rate to 4 per cent on the 31st July. More serious measures were soon found to be necessary. On the 5th September negotiations were opened with American and French banks with a view to raising a loan. Meanwhile the fall of sterling compelled the authorities to close the stock exchange and the bank rate was raised first to 5 per cent, and then to 6 per cent on the 25th September. Immediately afterwards came the news that it was impossible to raise a loan either in New York or in Paris. With its stock of gold reduced to 198 million kronor and its foreign exchange reserve to 30 millions, the Riksbank had reached the end of its tether, and on the 27th September Sweden left the gold standard. Simultaneously the discount rate was raised to 8 per cent as a precautionary measure against the possibility of an inflationary reaction and speculation in goods and foreign exchange.

THE SWEDISH BALANCE OF PAYMENTS 1930 AND 1931 (JAN.–SEPT.)[1] (In million kronor)

	January–June, 1930.	*July–December, 1930.*	*1930.*	*January–July, 1931.*	*July–September, 1931.*	*January–September, 1931.*
Foreign Trade—						
Exports	+ 737	+ 813	+ 1550	+ 493	+ 302	+ 795
Imports	− 829	− 835	− 1664	− 686	− 363	− 1049
Freight Incomes	+ 94	+ 95	+ 189	+ 70	+ 35	+ 105
	+ 2	+ 73	+ 75	− 123	− 26	− 149
Capital Movements—						
Export of Securities	+ 97	+ 101	+ 198	+ 166	+ 44	+ 210
Import of Securities	− 280	− 255	− 535	− 166	− 40	− 206
	− 183	− 154	− 337	0	+ 4	+ 4
Short-term Balances—						
Commercial Banks:						
Deposits	+ 145	− 7	+ 138	+ 85	− 237	− 152
Foreign Balances	+ 25	+ 32	+ 57	+ 20	+ 29	+ 49
	+ 170	+ 25	+ 159	+ 105	− 208	− 103
Items unaccounted for	+ 135	+ 57	+ 192	− 77	− 32	− 109
Grand total	+ 124	+ 1	+ 125	− 95	− 262	− 357
Foreign exchange Reserve of Riksbank (including bonds) Increase (+) Decrease (−)	+ 124	+ 1	+ 125	− 95	− 262	− 357

[1] Dr. Karin Kock, "Hur Sverige tvingades att överge guldmyntfoten," in Professor Myrdal's *Sveriges väg genom penningkrisen* (1931), p. 157.

Chapter VI

THE RECOVERY OF SWEDEN, 1933–5

(1) The Economists' Advice

THE situation immediately after the break from gold was full of ugly possibilities. All shades of opinion in Sweden were united in recognizing the need for drastic measures to prevent dangerous fluctuations in the value of the country's currency. The authorities lost no time in stating their future intentions. Throwing aside that reserve which is customary with Central Banks, the Riksbank joined with the Treasury in an official declaration which is unique. They announced that their policy would be to maintain the stability of the internal purchasing power of the krona in the hands of consumers. To prove that it meant business the bank also decided to equip itself with a new weapon, namely, an index of the weekly movement of the consumption price level. Professor Erik Lindahl undertook the task of working out its statistical basis. In this index the separate items are weighted according to their relative importance in the total consumption of the community. The initial weights were derived from an estimate of the aggregate consumption in Sweden in 1931 made by the Social Science Institute of the University of Stockholm. One series has a variable base, the current price level being compared with that of the preceding week: this offers an opportunity of adjusting the weights and the choice of goods to the trend of consumption. Another series relates the price changes to a fixed base—September, 1931—so as to give a continuous long-run picture. The index was created as a guide for the Central Bank and is to be regarded as a concrete corollary to its author's theory of monetary policy.

The following statement by Professor Lindahl is of interest. "The prices of raw materials, semi-manufactured and other capital goods which are produced during a given period admittedly do not enter so directly into the index in question. These prices must, however, stand in a certain relation to the prices of consumption goods, not indeed to those prevailing during the period in question, but to the prices which are expected to prevail during some future period when the capital goods have developed into products ready for consumption. General expectations as to the average development of prices of consumption goods during a series of future periods really provide the basis on which the price system in any given situation rests. By having an index constructed for the average change of consumption prices and by fixing the norms of monetary policy in relation to this index, a Central Bank furnishes the public with useful standpoints for estimating future price developments and this index will therefore be of fundamental importance to producers of capital goods. Owing to trade connections with foreign countries the situation will naturally be more complicated than is here described. If there is an alteration in the terms of trade with foreign countries and thus in the relation between export and import prices, a divergence may arise between the average prices of products and the average domestic consumption prices and it cannot be denied that for certain groups of producers, above all producers of export goods, an index series for the former prices would be of greater indirect importance than a consumption price index. It ought not, however, to be overlooked that this latter index is of considerable importance to the producers in question, both because it provides a standpoint for estimating certain items of costs, especially wages, and because under international conditions there must also be an intimate connection between the consumption price level and the product price level, since alterations in exchange relations only act as a modifying factor."[1] The new index

[1] Erik Lindahl, *The Consumption Price Index of the Bank of Sweden* (1933), p. 4.

number is clearly the offspring of neo-Wicksellian monetary theory; but whether it has been allowed to play any part in shaping Central Bank policy is a matter which can only be discussed in the light of other developments.

At the end of October and the beginning of November, 1931, a group of economists met in Stockholm to discuss the crisis; and the results of their deliberations were made available in Professor Myrdal's book *Methods of meeting the Monetary Crisis.*[1] Professor Heckscher's little volume *Sweden's Monetary Policy* appeared about the same time, and his proposals were in many ways similar to those of Professor Myrdal. Sweden was innocent of the breakdown of the international gold standard. Now that she was on a paper standard again, the problem was to choose the most effective methods of guaranteeing internal stability. The structure of relative prices inside the country would be continually disturbed by fluctuations in the rate of exchange. To meet these troubles it was obvious that the instrument of the discount rate would not itself suffice. Professor Myrdal emphasized that it was essential for the Central Bank to supplement it with other means of control. In times of monetary crisis a rise in the discount rate, instead of attracting short-term capital, often drives it away, because the bank's policy is

[1] *Sveriges väg genom penningkrisen* (1931).

interpreted by foreigners as a symptom of internal trouble. Thus we may well have the spectacle of short-term capital migrating from countries with high interest rates to those where rates are low. The risk factor is predominant. Moreover, speculation on the future exchange rate tends to exert greater influence on the volume of imports and stocks than variations in the rate of interest. The normal effect of bank rate changes on the volume of investment and stocks also loses its certainty. In Sweden it is usual for entrepreneurs to finance replacement and new investment by means of bank loans which they later pay off out of the proceeds of debenture issues. At a time when producers are full of uncertainty regarding the trend of short-term rates, it is manifestly out of the question to control the long-term rate through the discount rate. There is, further, the disconcerting possibility that a rise in the bank rate may even bolster up certain prices. Professor Myrdal instanced the situation in the real estate market where the short period elasticity of demand is low and capital cost is a relatively large part of total cost.[1] If builders are forced to cut down the supply of new houses, rents may be kept up rather than reduced. Many flats may be vacant, and their owners will not advertise for fear of disclosing their weak position. A revival of

[1] G. Myrdal, op. cit., p. 54 ff.

building activity will reduce rents; but a contraction will maintain them. As regards rents, a rise in the discount rate in such circumstances would not help to bring down the cost of living.

It may often be true that the rate of interest, considered merely as a cost item for the entrepreneur, will not be of much importance. But if the Central Bank declares that it will pursue a definite policy regarding the price level and use the discount rate accordingly, this very fact will influence entrepreneurs' anticipations. The course of the price level will then be determined by the expectations thus caused. It is, however, one thing to make an official declaration of policy and quite another to be able to carry it out effectively. A sudden movement of the exchange rate due to outside forces might well exercise an opposite effect on producers' anticipations. Both Professor Myrdal and Professor Heckscher stressed the fact that the public must have complete faith in the bank's intentions and in its capacity to fulfil them. In order to have the situation well in hand it would be necessary to resort to credit discrimination, e.g. to discourage imports; and the Central Bank would have to equip itself with a strong reserve of foreign exchange to be used to control movements of the exchange rate.

The contrast between two interpretations of

the depression was sharply revealed in a controversy between Professor Ohlin and Dr. Johan Åkerman.[1] According to Åkerman, who adopts the capital scarcity theory, it was vitally necessary to increase saving by reducing wages as well as rents and bond interest rates. He invoked statistical studies to prove that a rise in prices never starts in the retail trades but that the constructional industries first resume profitable working and the consequent increase in employment leads to a genuine rise in the demand for consumption goods. How to carry out a programme of general wage-cutting was, in his view, not an economic problem. He regarded the German device of Emergency Decrees as perhaps an extreme method which Sweden should not copy. A more expedient plan would be to conclude a national treaty reducing wages and money incomes by means of taxation. In Dr. Åkerman's opinion the world depression was complicated, as compared with previous slumps, by protectionist policies hindering liquidations, by the gap between monopolistic and free prices and by a weakening of the will to save. The situation called for international action to balance all budgets out of current revenue, and to secure general wage reductions, a

[1] See "Prisstegringens problem," in *Det ekonomiska läget*, 1932, No. 314. Also J. Åkerman, "Saving in the Depression," *Essays in Honour of Cassel*, pp. 11–31.

lowering of the 1921–9 interest rates, and the abolition of tariff barriers.

Professor Ohlin rejected the theoretical diagnosis upon which this policy was based. He emphasized the fact that increased saving does not guarantee a revival in real investment. It is uncertain whether it makes it cheaper or dearer to borrow. The immediate worsening of prospects in the consumption industries might mean that the added risk premium would more than offset the fall in the interest rate made possible by higher savings. Only harm can come from a rate of interest on the capital market which leads to savings running to waste. Finally, when there are unused resources it is not necessary to reduce the employment of labour and capital in the consumption goods industries in order to make new investment possible. The new savings are got partly out of the more complete use of existing capacity and are generated during the upward process itself.

The Swedish authorities did not act on Dr. Åkerman's advice; such a policy would probably have precipitated a disastrous deflation. We have seen in previous chapters that there is little theoretical justification for such a puritanical attitude; and the outcome of Dr. Brüning's heroic Emergency Decrees in Germany in 1931–2 is an apt commentary on its practical validity.

(2) Monetary Measures

With the suspension of the gold standard the krona-sterling rate jumped from 14·50 to 17·85 and went on rising till it reached par on the 17th November. The Riksbank, though its foreign exchange reserve was extremely meagre, decided to attempt to hold the rate at that level. But the pressure of foreign payments made this very difficult. It was found desirable to introduce a mild form of credit discrimination.[1] On the 21st November the Riksbank reached an agreement with the Swedish Bank Association to tighten up the conditions on which credits were granted for the financing of imports. This was an attempt to use the instrument of bank accommodation to restrict the volume of imports, increase the supply of foreign exchange, and prevent speculation. The Riksbank's supply of foreign exchange had fallen as low as 19 million kronor on the 21st November; but by the end of the year it had risen to 49 millions. In the first three months of the paper standard the gold value of the krona depreciated 30 per cent. Meanwhile conditions in the gold countries were worsening. Irving Fisher's wholesale price index for the United States, which stood at 104 in September, had fallen to 101 by December. The rise in wholesale prices in Sweden was negligible, namely,

[1] *Bankoutskottets memorial*, No. 1 (1931), p. 10.

from 107 to 111 in September–December, while the Riksbank's consumption price index showed hardly any change.

Up to the date when Sweden abandoned gold most prices were moving downwards. Afterwards the prices of certain imported goods tended to rise, particularly those purchased from gold countries, e.g. motor cars, writing materials, etc. In the case of purely domestic commodities the downward course of prices continued. The effect of the rise in the price of imports was offset by factors bringing about the decline of other prices. The falling off in the demand for Sweden's exports meant a considerable reduction in incomes in these branches of production, and this resulted in a lowering of the demand for consumers' goods. On the other hand, the rise in the krona prices of foreign goods gave a stimulus to home production in cases where similar commodities could be supplied within the country, e.g. textiles and motor cars. Where there was no such possibility, and the decrease in demand for the foreign commodity was less proportionately than the rise in price, the consumers' outlay on the imported commodity increased, so that they had less to spend on other things. Thus the rise in the prices of such imported goods was partly offset by a fall in the prices of other goods. The departure from gold did not send the prices of foreign goods soaring upwards. The average price level of imports rose only from 80 to 91 in the last quarter of 1931. One of the chief reasons for this was the progressive fall of prices in the gold countries.

The official monetary policy of the Central Bank received its first detailed interpretation in a statement issued by the Banking Committee of the Riksdag in May, 1932.[1] No attempt was to be made to tie the currency to the old gold parity, for that would involve serious deflationary measures. The internal price level and the needs of Swedish industry and trade would be the chief criteria of policy. It was desirable that the prices of home market products should rise, as long as the cost of living was not materially affected. The bank rate had been kept at 6 per cent until the 19th of February, 1932, and conditions were deemed at last favourable for a reduction. So the rate was brought down to 5 per cent by the 3rd of March. The shock of the Kreuger crisis of the 12th of March interfered with this policy, and it was only in May that a further reduction could take place. By the end of August the discount rate was down to 3½ per cent.

The strain of the unfavourable commodity balance in the first half of 1932 could not be ignored. The Riksbank, in lowering the discount rate in February, stipulated that credit

[1] *Bankoutskottets utlåtande*, No. 40 (1932).

discrimination against imports must be continued and this policy was not officially withdrawn until August, 1932. Fearing for their liquidity, the commercial banks were bound in any case to act cautiously. The following table shows the import surplus in the first three quarters of 1931 and 1932.

SWEDEN'S IMPORT SURPLUS (MILLION KRONOR)

	1931.	*1932.*
First Quarter . .	101	82
Second Quarter .	92	56
Third Quarter. .	61	42

There was little chance that the Central Bank would be able to carry out its declared policy, unless it could accumulate a large stock of foreign exchange. That it was able to increase its net holding of foreign exchange from 49 millions in December, 1931, to 213 millions in December, 1932, in a period when a large import surplus persisted, was a remarkable achievement. This was accomplished mainly through a large scale mobilization of the country's foreign assets. The following figures of imports and exports of securities bear this out.

IMPORTS AND EXPORTS OF SECURITIES [1] (MILLION KRONOR)

1932.	*Imports of Securities.*	*Exports of Securities.*	*Surplus.*
First Quarter .	20	59	39
Second Quarter .	21	31	10
Third Quarter .	21	45	24
Fourth Quarter .	21	63	42
	83	198	115

[1] *Bankoutskottets memorial,* No. 1 (1933), p. 7.

The Kreuger crash of 12th March was a temporary blow to confidence and the sterling-krona rate went up from 18·32 in March to 19·72 in April. No support was given to the market through sales of foreign exchange. At the end of May the rate on sterling was 19·50; and the Riksbank determined to hold it at that level. Meanwhile sterling went on depreciating in terms of the dollar, so that by August the krona had fallen to two-thirds of its gold value. The bank's considerable foreign exchange operations kept the sterling rate stable at 19·50; and this was undoubtedly the effect of the May declaration of the Banking Committee of the Riksdag. It was already clear that Sweden would strive to keep in line with sterling as long as this did not interfere with her internal policy.[1]

One can easily exaggerate the injury inflicted on Sweden by the Kreuger collapse. There are grounds for suggesting that perhaps on balance Kreuger did his country more good than harm. Technical efficiency increased considerably in the undertakings under his control. Moreover, before the international financial crisis, Kreuger had withdrawn large balances from Sweden; and this made the boom less speculative than it would otherwise have been. The sensation of his suicide and

[1] See also Professor B. Ohlin, *The Inadequacy of Price Stabilization*, Index (Stockholm), December, 1933, p. 256.

the discovery of his knavery led to a substantial depreciation of the krona in the spring of 1932, which was subsequently maintained. Without this, the deflation in that year would probably have been more severe.

The following table shows the course of some of the chief price indices in Sweden in 1932.

1932.	*Irving Fisher's wholesale price index, U.S.A.*	*Swedish wholesale prices.*	*Prices of imports.*	*Price of exports.*	*Riksbank's consumption price index.*
First Quarter . .	96	109	92	112	101·1
Second Quarter . .	92	109	92	109	101·3
Third Quarter . .	93	108	95	107	100·8
Fourth Quarter . .	91	109	97	108	101·4

There was a substantial fall in the average price of exports and a rise in the price of imports. The wholesale level and the Riksbank's consumption price index displayed a remarkable degree of stability, while wholesale prices in the United States continued to fall. Business conditions, however, went from bad to worse. The index of the volume of production fell during 1932 from 97 to 87 and the proportion of trade unionists registered as unemployed reached the high average of 25 per cent in the last quarter.

In September, 1932, a Labour Government under the leadership of Mr. Per Albin Hansson took office. The depression was at its worst, and the capacity of the new administration was put sorely to the test. It soon became obvious that the Finance Minister, Mr. Wigforss, was determined to use the budget as an instrument of recovery. He was no believer in the efficacy of nature's cure. New inspiration was also communicated to the Riksbank; and early in 1933 a representative Committee of economists, civil servants, bankers, and business men was appointed to consider future monetary policy and a unanimous report was presented in May.[1] Much greater emphasis was now laid on the desirability of a rise in the internal price level. Since the items in the cost of living were largely independent of the wholesale price level, the danger of a rise in the cost of living could be ignored. Even fears regarding the consequences of a fall in the external value of the currency were slurred over as subsidiary. The main consideration was to create a safe margin for an independent effort to re-employ idle factors of production. National and municipal budgetary policies should go hand in hand with the Central Bank's monetary measures in order to realize this end. So long as the fall in the krona's external value did not exceed the rise in the internal price level, the experts saw no objection to it. The Government rigorously set its hands to the task of co-ordinating monetary and budget policy; and before the end of 1933 the forces making for recovery had been considerably accelerated.

[1] See K. M.'s *Proposition*, No. 260 (1933), p. 13 ff. An account of the purely monetary measures up to 1933 is given in E. T. H. Kjellstrom, *Managed Money: the Experience of Sweden* (New York, 1934).

The remarkable stability of the cost of living between 1931 and 1933 strengthened the hands of the Government in its effort to secure a rise in wholesale prices. The official policy contemplated neither an early return to gold nor a pegging of the sterling rate of exchange: the external value of the krona was to be allowed to adjust itself to the internal purchasing power. Any depreciation for the purpose of gaining competitive advantages was to be avoided.

The way was paved for a fall in rates of interest by negotiations conducted by the Riksbank with the savings banks. When the latter had consented to adjust their deposit rates, the Central Bank was able to reduce the discount rate by ½ per cent to 3 per cent in June, 1933. After a lag of a few months the commercial banks in September decided to bring down their rates by ½ per cent. The Central Bank, in view of the situation of the private banks, purchased a large amount of securities during the autumn; and in December, 1933, reduced its discount rate again by ½ to 2½ per cent. The savings banks now resolved as from the beginning of 1934 to lower their deposit rate to 3 per cent. Meanwhile the long-term rate of interest reached 3·71 per cent at the end of 1933 compared with 4·01 per cent at the close of the previous year.

Cheap money made no impression on the rate of borrowing during 1933. The volume of rediscounts by the commercial banks at the Riksbank reached a record low level.[1] Better conditions in the export trade brought the import surplus down to 11 million kronor compared with 207 million in 1932; and this led to a piling up of foreign exchange in the Central Bank. By the end of 1933 the stock of foreign exchange held by the Riksbank reached the total of 657 million kronor (at current rates), and there was a net addition of 146 millions to the gold reserve. Another cause of this development was the continuance of the net export of securities. Having been so successful in 1932 in building up a strong reserve of foreign exchange, the Bank became concerned about the erratic fluctuations in exchange rates. The departure of the United States from the gold standard at the end of April, 1933, had rather disturbing consequences. The dollar-sterling rate jumped from 3·58 in April to 4·04 in June; and during the same months the krona-sterling rate moved from 19·06 to 19·46. The Riksbank was determined to prevent the krona rate from falling back and sought to hold it stable at 19·40 by dominating the foreign exchange market. This was in line with official monetary policy. During 1933 prices began to rise in countries with paper standards; and, if this was to prove beneficial to Sweden, it was important to keep

[1] *Bankoutskottets memorial*, No. 1, January, 1934, p. 8.

the sterling rate stable—particularly as the dollar was falling in relation to the pound. Any appreciation of the Swedish currency in terms of sterling would have been a serious drag on internal recovery. The measures necessary to prevent this were burdensome, but the authorities made it clear that considerations of profit were subsidiary to the larger end of providing a suitable margin for recovery.[1] The net surplus earned by the bank in 1933 was 10·6 million kronor compared with 14·5 millions in 1932.

A further statement by the Riksbank in April, 1934, clarified some of the motives underlying its policy of maintaining a stable rate on sterling. The authorities took the view that it was vital for the Swedish export industries to take full advantage of the slow recovery in the world at large. Stability of the sterling rate was a powerful method of minimizing the difficulties in the international money markets. As a practical result, exporters found it less necessary to insure against exchange risks, whereas commercial banks held a larger proportion of their short-term assets in sterling. During 1934 the discount rate remained at 2½ per cent, and the savings banks' deposit rate fell to an average of 2·9 per cent in November. The bank's foreign exchange reserve at the end of 1934 stood at the high level of 519

[1] *Bankoutskottets memorial*, No. 1, 16th January, 1934, p. 13.

million kronor and its gold holdings at 350 millions. Since the krona-sterling exchange was held stable at the rate of 19·40, the Swedish currency underwent the same fluctuations as sterling in relation to other currencies. The active measure taken by the Central Bank in 1933 and 1934 did much to provide the framework within which recovery could become effective.

(3) The Budget and Public Works [1]

The Swedish budget draws a distinction between ordinary or current expenditure and expenditure on additions to national assets. Some of the latter items are financed in the Ordinary Budget and others in the Loan Budget. The rules of financial orthodoxy decree that the State can use borrowed money only for investments that are "productive", i.e. self-liquidating in the market sense. The State owns the railways, telegraphs, and one-quarter of the country's forests. Among the "State Productive Funds" are the shares held in a large iron ore company and in the public monopolies controlling tobacco and spirits. The "State Loan Funds" enable credit to be

[1] I am indebted to the editor of *The Economist* for permission to incorporate in this and the following section passages from two articles contributed to that journal, namely "Another Public Works Budget", 27th January, 1934, and "Changes in Swedish Banking", Banking Supplement, 12th May, 1934.

granted on liberal conditions for objects of social or national importance, e.g. housing and railway development. The Bank of Sweden is a publicly owned institution: its profits appear separately in the budget accounts and are not included with Income from Public Enterprise.

The chief sources of revenue to be hit by the slump were the taxes on income and property, the customs, stamp duties, and the State railways and domains. The following table gives details regarding the yield of taxes and public enterprise incomes in the period 1929–30 to 1933–4.

REVENUE FROM TAXES AND PUBLIC ENTERPRISE[1] (MILLION KRONOR)

	1929–30.	*1930–31.*	*1931–32.*	*1932–33.*	*1933–34.*
Taxes, Customs, and Excise.					
Income and Property Tax	146·0	160·4	157·4	132·3	127·5
Stamp Duties	54·9	56·8	48·8	49·7	49·7
Motor car tax	44·3	51·4	58·8	72·8	78·5
Customs	154·5	147·5	137·5	117·2	113·4
Tobacco Tax	69·8	65·8	70·1	72·9	74·8
Alcoholic Drink Taxes	110·1	107·1	113·8	139·3	143·6
State Productive Funds.					
Post Office	14·6	15·3	14·6	13·2	16·5
Telegraphs	23·4	26·1	26·5	28·2	30·8
Railways	46·9	36·9	15·9	11·4	4·2
Waterworks	17·5	16·4	16·3	16·6	16·9
Domains	13·3	11·6	3·9	7·0	10·1
Luossavaara-Kiirunavaara Iron Ore Company:[2]	11·5	12·6	6·2	−1·4	—
Tobacco Monopoly	3·8	8·1	1·6	1·6	11·6

During the three years 1931–2 to 1933–4 when the depression was acute, the yield of stamp duties was maintained constant, that of the motor car tax was considerably increased, and

[1] *Riksräkenskapsverkets inkomberäkning for budgetåret, 1935–6* (1935), p. 4.

[2] The share capital of this company is 80 million kronor, half of which are preference shares owned by the State.

the rise in the revenue from alcoholic drinks due to steep increases in tax rates was actually enough to make up for the decline in the yield of the income and property tax. The profits obtained from the post office, telegraphs, and waterworks also proved remarkably buoyant.

The main interest of Sweden's budgetary history in recent years is the experiment that was made by Mr. Wigforss, the Labour Finance Minister, of using the budget to induce industrial revival. It was essential to secure co-operation between the Treasury and the Riksbank, for monetary policy in the narrow sense cannot succeed unless it is co-ordinated with measures undertaken in the sphere of public finance. The fundamental problem was whether the budget was to be balanced in the orthodox manner, year by year, by rigid economy and a stiffening of tax rates, accompanied by a deflation of wage incomes, or whether the budget should temporarily be unbalanced by a resort to loan-expenditure. Nominal wages in 1933 had fallen only by 5 per cent compared with the 1930 level, while, with the lowering of the cost of living, real wages per hour were actually higher in 1932 than in 1929. Any attempt to enforce a considerable cut in wages would have been met by powerful resistance and the threat of social upheaval. The predecessors of the Labour Government had been compelled to admit this, for the budgets of 1931–2 and 1932–3 had only been balanced by the help of a raid to the tune of 165 million kronor on the reserves of the Alcoholic Drink Account. This was really nothing but a veiled species of "under-balancing". Mr. Wigforss, however, did not hesitate to proclaim his unorthodoxy openly. In his first budget estimate of January, 1933, he decided to borrow 160 million kronor to finance public works which are not self-liquidating and to raise the death duties to yield 40 million kronor to provide for the amortization of the special loans within four years. To quote his words, "the budget is based on the assumption that the international situation will undergo no appreciable change and that in Sweden there will be no spontaneous tendency towards recovery, except to the extent that the policy of the State will help to bring it about. . . . In seeking to achieve this object, the State's financial policy must obviously play an important part." [1] He declared himself to be in agreement with the theoretical argument propounded in Professor Myrdal's memorandum on "Budget Policy and the Trade Cycle" which was published as a supplement to the budget estimates. The plan was adopted by the Riksdag with slight modifications to meet opposition from conservative quarters. The

[1] *Bilagor till 1933 års statsverksproposition* (1933), pp. 8–9.
[2] *Konjunktur och offentliga hushållning* (1933).

sum to be borrowed was reduced by 10 million kronor and the amortization period extended from four to five years.

A stoppage in the building industry broke out in April, 1933, and lasted for the rest of the year. This proved embarrassing for the Government's programme and weakened its beneficial effects in the early stages. The Minister appreciated the limits to an induced expansion set by the external value of the currency and by the desire not to see the cost of living rise. But he pointed out that, if the early effects would call for a shrinkage of consumption or a curtailment of imports in order to increase the supply of savings, protect the currency, and put the brake on an undesirable rise in prices, then the authorities would interfere by taxing consumption or regulating foreign trade. Subsequent events showed such safeguards to be unnecessary; but danger appeared from another quarter. The commercial banks took a dislike to the Labour Government's budget proposals; and their prejudice expressed itself in a sudden tightening tendency in the capital market. The long-term rate of interest, as measured by the effective yield of bonds had been steadily falling during 1932 (except for a temporary reaction due to the Kreuger crash) and reached 4·0 per cent in November. Then between November, 1932, and April, 1933, it rose again to 4·27 per cent.

This was the very time when the Treasury announced the scope of its large-scale programme of loan-expenditure. There could not have been much co-operation between the Finance Ministry and the Riksbank at that stage. Fortunately it was only a passing phase and the long-term rate renewed its downward course and reached 3·71 per cent by the end of 1933.

The Government's second budget, tabled in January, 1934, provided for further borrowing to the amount of 120 million kronor to be spent on " unproductive " public works.[1] As cover for amortization 26 millions were to be obtained from death duties, 8 millions from a new surtax on large properties and incomes, and 6 millions from a stamp duty on estates. The redemption period was extended to seven years. The Minister was of the view that, as the depression had worked itself out and the forces making for recovery were still weak, a large volume of loan-financed public investment would be of the utmost value. He saw no necessity, particularly in view of the fluid state of the money market, for deflating ordinary expenditure or increasing current taxation, in order to accommodate it.

The art of balancing the budget in a depression is chiefly a matter of skilfully sugaring the pill without arousing undue

[1] *Bilagor till 1934 års statsverksproposition* (1934).

suspicion. It is rare, however, to find a Finance Minister going out of his way to disclose the precise kind of sugar he has used and the thickness with which he has laid it on. But this is exactly what Mr. Wigforss did in the statement accompanying the 1934 budget estimates. He took great pains to point out that some of his important savings were really fictitious, as they were the result of such expedients as dropping sinking-fund payments for certain purposes, suspending contributions to pension funds, and transferring various small items to the Loan Budget. These elastic ways of securing budgetary equilibrium were equivalent to putting the burden on the Loan Budget. Such frankness in a budget statement is refreshing. It proves either that Swedish public opinion is so sophisticated that such shocks leave it cold or that it is so indifferent that no harm is done.

A glance at Table I will show the effect of the public works policy on the relative importance of the Loan Budget. Aggregate expenditure, taking the Ordinary and the Loan Budgets together, grew continuously from 779·31 million kronor in 1929–1930 to 1,106·35 millions in 1934–5, an increase of 42 per cent. In the four financial years 1928–9 to 1931–2 a little over one-twentieth of the total expenditure was met by borrowing; but in the two years 1933–4 to

1934–5 no less than one-quarter of the aggregate was financed in the Loan Budget. New loan-expenditure for non-self-liquidating public works constituted 15 per cent of the total budget in 1933–4.

True to his conception of the role of budgetary policy in the trade cycle, the Finance Minister framed his estimates for 1935–6 without any extraordinary loan expenditure. The purpose had been served. His two previous budgets had contributed to the substantial recovery experienced in 1934. A period of "under-balancing" must be followed by years of cautious finance. The 1935 budget, though it did not raise any taxes, provided for the expenditure of 50 millions on public works to be paid for out of current revenue. Expenditure in the Loan Budget was 136·6 millions compared with 282·1 in 1934–5.

The budget proposals for 1936–7 are an eloquent proof of the success of the Treasury's policy.[1] The income tax is reduced by 12 per cent, and the loans which were incurred to finance public investment are to be wholly repaid. Mr. Wigforss, in the statement accompanying the estimates, points out that the total sum borrowed for public works was 300 million kronor, of which 103 millions have already been amortized. The funds for paying off the

[1] *Bilaga till 1936 års statsverksproposition : Inkomsterna*, pp. 15–29.

remainder are to be obtained as follows: 38 millions from the tax on large incomes and property earmarked for the purpose, 59 millions from cash reserves, 12 millions from the Government's share-holdings, and 7 millions from the yield of the motor car tax. The experiment of using the budget as an instrument of expansionist policy has thus been abundantly justified; and the experience of this new technique will be of great advantage to Sweden in dealing with future crises.

(4) The State and the Banks

The Kreuger crash brought to the forefront the question of tightening the State's control over the banking system. The public reacted to the sensational collapse with remarkable equipoise; but all parties agreed in regarding it as a painful object-lesson proving that further legal restrictions on the banks were necessary. Accordingly the Riksdag on the 2nd June, 1933, passed an important law amending the 1911 Bank Act; and it entered into force on the 1st January, 1934.

In assessing its significance it is important to realize the part which the banks have hitherto played in financing industry. Swedish investors have only since the War acquired the habit of putting their money directly into shares or bonds. They have generally preferred to have time deposits in the commercial or savings banks. Moreover, since Sweden has no open money market in the English sense, business men with temporary surplus funds have no alternative to placing them in the bank. Since the War they have been able to use a special account liable to fourteen days' notice and thus receive a higher rate of interest than the ½ per cent obtainable on current account. In such circumstances the banks inevitably became the suppliers not only of short term credits but also of investment capital for the country's rapidly expanding industries. Loans are nominally granted for a maximum period of six months; but in practice most of them are renewed and run for years. It has been usual for a newly formed company to supplement its own capital with renewable bank credits and repay them later out of the proceeds of a debenture issue. The War-time inflationary boom revealed the weakness of this system. The banks formed subsidiary investment companies and placed large credits at their disposal. Reckless flotation and merging of dubious concerns by these companies caused the banks heavy losses. The practice of making advances on the security of shares assumed excessive proportions and in the severe post-War slump the banks were left with many firms virtually on their hands. It is one of the evils of the Swedish method of financing industry that the banks are tempted to keep uneconomic enterprises on their feet rather than undergo the certain loss of liquidating them.

A committee was appointed in 1924 to examine the relations of the banks to industry. Its report, which appeared in 1927, proposed far-reaching alterations in the bank law.[1] But by that time the frozen credits had been liquidated and industrial companies were financially much sounder ; so the whole matter was quietly shelved. In the boom of 1927–9 the banks were more cautious, though the business of lending against shares again became prominent. The depression was accompanied by the disturbing Kreuger collapse in March, 1932, which involved one of the largest banks, Skandinaviska Kreditaktiebolaget, in serious difficulties. The Government was obliged to grant it assistance to the amount of 215 million kronor ; and the Riksdag coupled its approval with an emphatic declaration that stricter public control over the banking system was highly desirable. A committee was appointed to re-examine the connection betweeen the banks and industry ; and the Labour Government used its report as the basis for the new law which is now in force. The Kreuger affair was thus the immediate cause of the demand for new legislation ; but it is pertinent to add that, even if the crash had not occurred, the slump would have seriously affected some of the banks.

[1] *Betänkande med förslag till lag om ändring i vissa delar av lagen den 22 Juni 1911 om bankrörelse* (Official Publications, 1927, No. 11).

The general principle which has always characterized Swedish bank legislation is that the interests of the depositor must be adequately protected. The scope of the new law gives the impression that henceforth the banking system will have to work within a rigid strait-jacket. But it must be remembered that many of its provisions have been in operation for years. Among the novel features are the important restrictions placed on the banks' power of granting credits, though some of them were already contained in Articles of Association. The fundamental provision is that no credit may be given without adequate security in the form of real or movable property or in claims against a third party. The business of lending against shares is severely curtailed. There must be an appreciable margin between the market value of the shares and the amount of the loan, and this must be maintained. It is forbidden to make advances against the shares of a company which deals in shares or undertakes issuing business. The renewal of a credit is regarded as a new loan. To avoid friction the operation of these clauses is subject to transitional arrangements. The banks must, further, refrain from granting credits to financially interconnected enterprises on such a scale as to endanger liquidity; and the same rule applies to advances made on the security of the shares of such companies. The bank's limited right to acquire shares, according to the 1911 Act, has now been abolished.

Another section seeks to ensure that credit policy shall not be influenced by personal considerations. Loans must not be granted to directors, high officials, and auditors of the bank nor to an undertaking with which such persons are intimately connected, except on the security of gilt-edged bonds or equivalent collateral. An exception is made in favour of such a company's commercial bills. Furthermore no bank director or official may be simultaneously a member of the board of an enterprise dealing in shares or engaged in issuing business. Detailed provisions are inserted to counteract the practice whereby important decisions are delegated by the Board of Directors to subordinate authorities. The law enumerates various matters, e.g. the buying and selling of real estate, interest policy, and the granting of specific kinds of credits, for which the Board is to be held solely responsible.

This close network of restrictions is completed by an exhaustive statement of the powers of the Bank Inspectorate. This State authority has the duty of seeing that banks carry on their business in accordance with the Bank Law, their Articles of Association, and the resolutions of the Board and general meeting; and it publishes regular statistics. Its functions are now made much more explicit. Hitherto, the inspection, which is an elaborate affair lasting several months, has taken place about once every three years ; in future it is expected to occur at least every other year. The Inspectorate has the right to demand from the banks any information which bears on its task. It may propose to the Government measures calculated to facilitate supervisions, and may report any bank guilty of abuses. It has the right at any time to summon the Board of Directors or a meeting of the shareholders. There are one or two instances where the Board of a bank has actually been convened. Finally, the Inspectorate can invoke the co-operation of the Riksbank, a possibility which might be significant if it implied that the Central Bank would use its power of bringing pressure to bear on a recalcitrant bank.

There can be no doubt that the new legislation has the active support of the mass of Swedish public opinion. It is not without interest that the Association of Banks confined its major criticisms to the curtailment of the right to acquire and lend against shares. Meanwhile the problem of devising suitable machinery for financing certain types of long-term investment has still to be faced. Indeed the effect of the new dispensation is to emphasize the deficiencies in the structure of the Swedish capital market. A new institute has, therefore, been created to meet the demand for long- and middle-term credits. An Expert Committee proposed that a start should be made with a share capital of 8 million kronor, of which 5 millions are to be subscribed by the State and the remainder by the banks, together with a State guarantee fund of 12 millions in Government stock. The Institute is to have the right to issue bonds up to four times the amount of the capital guarantee and the reserve fund to be formed later. The basis for its operations is thus fixed at 60 million kronor. The long-term credits contemplated are those over ten years and the middle-term from one to ten years. Risky investments are to be avoided, and the quality of the security is to weigh more than the probable effect on employment. The Institute may in certain cases take over old bank credits if this makes it easier for the bank to grant further accommodation while not involving the Institute in excessive risk. Its activity is designed to provide a stimulus to new investment and rationalization, as well as easier credit conditions for the export trades and small- and middle-sized enterprises. It is calculated specially to satisfy the requirements of those undertakings which, by reason of their structure or the nature of their business, are unable to avail themselves of the bond market. The State, having interfered to keep the banks within what it considers to be their legitimate sphere of action, must logically take the initiative in furnishing the needs of the long-term capital market. In view of the traditions of the Swedish money and capital markets, it will be interesting to see whether this experiment will prove to be an adequate solution.

(5) The Extent of the Recovery

The upward turn seems to have begun in the first half of 1933. Since then there has been an unmistakable expansion which has carried the level of economic activity beyond that of the prosperous year 1929. The index of the volume of production rose from 85 in the second quarter of 1933 to 119 in the second quarter of 1935. The increase of physical production in the home market industries in this period was from 90 to 128, and in the export trades from 76 to 100. The wholesale price level has been rising consistently since the middle of 1933 (from 106 to 115). A glance at the prices of foreign trade goods shows that the terms of trade have been moving in Sweden's favour. The average price of imports has risen slowly, but that of exports in 1933 and 1934 has risen faster. It is an interesting fact that the favourable demand for Swedish products, which we noted in our analysis of the pre-1929 boom, has also been a strong factor in the recovery of 1933–5. A comparison with the pre-War terms of trade lends colour to the view that the secular trend is in favour of Swedish exports. In the

SWEDEN
(Annual averages)

A=Cost of Living (Socialstyrelsen index, July 1914=100)
B=Wholesale Prices (Kommerskollegium index, 1913=100)

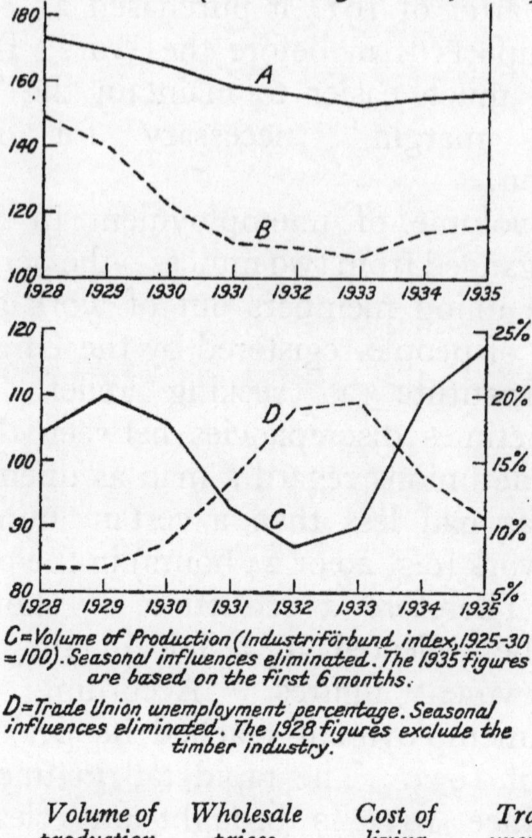

C=Volume of Production (Industriförbund index, 1925-30 =100). Seasonal influences eliminated. The 1935 figures are based on the first 6 months.

D=Trade Union unemployment percentage. Seasonal influences eliminated. The 1928 figures exclude the timber industry.

	Volume of production (1925–30 = 100).	*Wholesale prices* (1913 = 100.	*Cost of living* (July, 1914 = 100).	*Trade Union unemployment percentage.*
1928 .	104	148	173	6·9
1929 .	110	140	169	6·9
1930 .	106	122	164	8·6
1931 .	93	111	158	13·2
1932 .	87	109	156	19·0
1933 .	90	107	153	19·4
1934 .	110	114	155	14·0
1935 .	118	116	156	10·9

Source : *Ekonomisk Översikt*, issued by the Swedish Board of Trade.

third quarter of 1928 and 1929 each unit of Swedish exports exchanged for 15 per cent more imports than it did in 1913; but in the third quarter of 1934 it purchased 25 per cent more imports than before the War. This has made it much easier to maintain the "international margin" necessary for internal expansion.

The volume of unemployment in Sweden may be gauged from two indices—the percentage of trade union members out of work and the number of people registered by the Unemployment Institute as seeking relief. There are sometimes discrepancies between the two. The trade unions regard a man as unemployed if he has had less than a certain number of hours' work (e.g. 20 or 24 hours) in the previous week. Therefore a reduction of short time would be reflected in a fall in the unions' unemployment figures. According to this index, unemployment reached its peak in the spring of 1933. The rapid fall in unemployment since 1933 is brought out clearly by both indices. The proportion of trade unionists out of work in the third quarter of 1935 was only 10 per cent compared with 25 per cent in the corresponding quarter of 1933. The absolute total of unemployed registered by the Institute diminished from a maximum of 189,000 at the beginning of 1933 to 50,000 in the third quarter of 1935.

Emergency relief works are undertaken in Sweden to cope with abnormal unemployment, and the wages paid are about 15 per cent below trade union rates. When the Government embarked on extensive schemes of public investment financed by loans, the Labour Party and the trade unions insisted that wages in these contracts should be equal to the rate which an unskilled trade unionist could claim in the district where the work was provided. The fear that labourers would be attracted away from agriculture proved unfounded. This policy was quite justified. If the unemployed are put on to a temporary piece of relief work in the interests of their physique, it is not unreasonable that their earnings should be lower than what they would obtain in an ordinary job. But there is no reason why the State should pay its permanent staff of unskilled workers less than the market rate.

The level of industrial wages has not altered much since 1929. The average rate per hour fell from 286 in 1930 to 270 in 1934, the rate per day from 241 to 227, and the rate per annum from 233 to 220. Real wages per hour in 1934 were 75 per cent above 1913 compared with 80 per cent in 1930; real wages per annum actually rose from 42 to 43 per cent above the pre-War year.[1] The cuts of 1931 and 1932 brought money wages down by only about

[1] *Sociala Meddelanden*, 1935, No. 6, p. 375.

5 per cent. The earnings of the workers in private industry were well maintained, and they were supplemented by the State expenditure on public works. According to Professor Ohlin, " in the situation ruling in 1932 it would have been useless to wait for an increase in investment demand to follow a fall in wages costs. It was an important circumstance that the tendencies towards deflation which lasted, though in a weakened form, did not get the support of large wage reductions."[1]

The Government had to take steps to alleviate the burdens of agricultural producers. This was not only a part of the general policy of raising wholesale prices; it was also the reward of the Farmers' Party for supporting the Labour Administration. The State every year purchases all home grown corn of the previous harvest at a guaranteed price (wheat 19 kronor per metric quintal); and a limit is set on the amount of foreign corn which flour mills may use. The serious problem of surplus milk and butter had also to be met. Farmers pay a tax on all milk retailed to the consumer. Margarine is taxed at the rate of 0·34 kronor per kilogramme, and the price of butter in Sweden is fixed at 2·30 kronor per kilogramme. Most of the yield of these taxes is handed over to the exporters of butter to make up for the difference between its internal and export

[1] Ohlin, *International Labour Review*, May, 1935, p. 690.

price. It is estimated that this scheme added 23 million kronor to the value of the butter sold to Swedish consumers in 1934. To prevent the artificially high price from stimulating production, the Government increased the farmers' costs by levying a tax on oil-cake. Imports of sugar are regulated by a monopoly in the interests of the home industry. These measures meant an increase of between 15 and 20 per cent in the income of farmers in the years 1932–4.[1]

Investment

The national income of Sweden increased from 6,350 million to 7,200 million kronor between 1932 and 1934. It is estimated that a half of the new income was devoted to the production of capital goods the value of which rose by 10 per cent. This brought the rate of investment up to three-quarters of the 1929 level. Retail prices have been stable; the amount spent on consumption goods increased by 10 per cent.

The revival in investment is seen clearly in the iron and steel and the building industries. The production of iron ore and pig iron is shown in the table on p. 226.[2] The output of iron ore in 1934 was double that of 1933, though it was still only half of

[1] Ohlin, loc. cit., p. 686 ff.
[2] *Kommersiella Meddelanden*, 1935, No. 9.

what it was in 1930. The production of pig iron, on the other hand, was well above

OUTPUT (TONS)

	Iron Ore.	Pig Iron.
1913 . .	7,476,000	730,207
1930 . .	11,236,000	459,780
1931 . .	7,071,000	389,236
1932 . .	3,299,000	264,775
1933 . .	2,699,000	323,073
1934 . .	5,253,000	524,781

1930. It is in iron and steel products that recovery has been most marked as the following figures show.

AVERAGE MONTHLY OUTPUT [1] (1,000 TONS)

	Wrought Iron and Steel.	Rolling Mill Products.
1913 . .	62·4	38·8
1929 . .	59·8	42·0
1930 . .	52·4	34·8
1931 . .	45·5	33·3
1932 . .	44·6	32·2
1933 . .	53·4	38·8
1934 . .	72·8	51·9
1935 . .	74·0 [2]	52·0 [2]

There was a record output of both wrought iron and steel and rolling mill products in 1935, the increase compared with the lowest point of the slump being 64 and 62 per cent respectively. The pace has slowed down in 1935. Sweden produces two kinds of iron and steel, the high-grade quality for export and ordinary iron used, for example, in building. The latter has recovered more rapidly that the former owing to the boom in the home market.

Building in Sweden gives employment

[1] *Kommersiella Meddelanden*, 1935, No. 21.

[2] The first nine months.

directly and indirectly to 12 per cent of the industrial population (excluding agriculture and fisheries). The total number of building operatives rose from 70,000 in 1910 to 165,000 in 1930. A long stoppage paralysed this industry for the best part of 1933; and it was not until work was resumed in February, 1934, that the public works programme of the Government was given a fair chance. There are statistics of the number of rooms in buildings which are completed each quarter, and of the number of permits issued.

SWEDEN

Indices of Building Activity (Eleven towns: Number of rooms in (*a*) buildings for which permits have been issued; (*b*) buildings completed).

		Permits.	*Completed.*
1929		100·0	100·0
1930		107·4	134·2
1931		85·9	132·2
1932		76·8	118·9
1933		47·9	79·4
1934		102·0	92·3
1934:	First Quarter	72·3	56·1
	Second Quarter	104·6	24·0
	Third Quarter	89·2	176·1
	Fourth Quarter	141·7	113·1
1935:	First Quarter	169·6	103·6
	Second Quarter	142·0	43·4
	Third Quarter	84·1	274·4

The table shows that a building boom began in the second half of 1934 and it has continued unabated. The number of dwellings built in the eleven largest towns in the third quarter of 1935 was 7,660, or an increase of 52 per cent over the corresponding period of 1934.[1]

[1] *Sociala Meddelanden*, 1935, No. 11, p. 760.

Costs in this industry are extremely rigid. Between 1928 and 1934 wages fell by only 4 per cent and the prices of building materials by 15 per cent. But the long-term rate of interest was reduced by 35 per cent. " The statistics for Sweden and the United Kingdom go to show that a considerable rigidity of both the prices of materials and wages is not necessarily an obstacle to building activity if there is a sharp fall in the long term rate of interest." [1]

The Balance of Payments

The Swedish balance of payments for 1933 and 1934 has very interesting features.[2] The value of commodity exports rose by 21 per cent (from 1,093 million kronor to 1,319 millions) and that of imports by 19 per cent (from 1,108 millions to 1,319 millions). A visible deficit of 58 millions was turned into a surplus of 78 millions. The invisible items gave a net credit balance of 216 millions in 1934 compared with 227 millions in the previous year. Thus, on income account, the positive balance increased from 169 millions to 294 millions. The capital account shows that the export of securities declined in 1934 compared with 1933 while the import of foreign securities was larger.

[1] *World Economic Survey* (*League of Nations Economic Service*), 1934–5, p. 65.

[2] See Table III in the Statistical Appendix.

The international margin provided favourable conditions for the Government's recovery programme. In spite of the increase in the demand for consumption goods due to home market activity, the position was even more satisfactory in 1934 than in 1933. The greater need for imported commodities was more than offset by the expansion of the export trade.

The exports of iron-ore increased from 507,000 tons in the last quarter of 1932, to 1,466,000 tons in the corresponding period of 1934. Engineering normally exports one-third of its output and is, therefore, very susceptible to conditions in foreign markets. The trade union index of employment in this industry moved from 70·8 to 86·8 per cent. A similar improvement was experienced by the other export trades, for example, paper, pulp, and timber.

During 1935, however, commodity exports ceased to expand, while imports showed a considerable increase over the previous year, as shown by the following figures.[1]

THE TRADE BALANCE AND CAPITAL MOVEMENTS

January to November, 1935 (million kronor).

	Imports.	*Exports.*		*Imports of Securities.*	*Exports of Securities.*		*Total Import Surplus − Export Surplus +.*
1934	1,189	1,155	−34	125	114	−21	−55
1935	1,333	1,163	−170	100	113	+13	−157

This development is a natural result of prosperity in the home market; and there is no reason to regard it as a threat to the stability

[1] *Bankoutskottets memorial 1936*, No. 1, p. 5.

of the recovery. It will simply mean that in 1936 the enormous foreign exchange reserve of the Riksbank, which amounted to 629 million kronor at the end of 1935, will undergo a slight reduction.

Bank Credit

The volume of bank clearings is a useful barometer of industrial activity.

INDEX OF BANK CLEARINGS[1] (SEASONAL CHANGES ELIMINATED)
(*Skandinaviska Kreditaktiebolaget*)
(1929 = 100)

Quarter.	*1932.*	*1933.*	*1934.*
I . . .	78·7	70·8	88·0
II . . .	69·7	71·5	86·7
III . . .	69·2	77·1	89·0
IV . . .	68·1	77·3	87·1

According to these figures industrial revival began in the second half of 1933. The position of the Riksbank and the commercial banks is shown in the following table[2]:—

THE RIKSBANK AND THE COMMERCIAL BANKS

	31st December, 1933.	*31st July, 1934.*	*31st December, 1934.*	*31st July, 1935.*
		(*million kronor*)		
The Riksbank.				
Gold Reserve . .	370·3	371·2	351·3	356·5
Foreign Exchange .	446·2	457·0	553·4	622·3
Home Advances .	56·3	38·2	43·6	43·8
Note Circulation .	647·6	611·8	708·2	685·5
Deposits in Current Accounts (excluding Public Deposits) .	248·5	308·3	196·1	291·2
The Commercial Banks.				
Deposits . . .	3628·7	3628·9	3552·7	3691·7
Advances :				
Loans and Credits .	2802·0	2734·1	2749·4	2815·5
Bills . . .	1103·4	1065·9	1045·4	1065·0
Rediscounting at Riksbank . .	0·5	—	—	0·1
Excess of Advances .	277·2	171·1	242·1	188·9
Excess of Claims on Abroad . . .	106·4	187·7	224·6	190·9

[1] Dr. Karin Kock, *Konjunkturuppsvingets förlopp och orsaker, 1932–4*, Official Publications, 1935, No. 16, p. 26.

[2] The *Swedish Economic Review*, June and September, 1935.

It is interesting to note the appreciable rise in the Riksbank's foreign exchange reserve and in the note circulation. The deposits of the commercial banks showed an increase in July, 1935, compared with the previous year. Loans and credits at the end of 1934 were lower than in December, 1933. Old bank loans were being repaid faster than new credits were being absorbed. The almost complete absence of rediscounting at the Central Bank demonstrates how fluid the money market has remained.

(6) The Nature of the Recovery

Nothing succeeds like success. Sweden's spectacular recovery has been hailed by some monetary reformers as proof of the validity of their particular doctrines. Professor Irving Fisher is so impressed that he calls upon the poor deluded world to turn for guidance to the little Scandinavian kingdom. "Whatever the future holds in store," he writes, "this achievement of Sweden will always be the most important landmark up to its time in the history of stabilization ; and the various efforts which have been made to discredit the importance of Sweden's example can never erase the simple fact that Sweden *did* stabilize the internal purchasing power of her krona according to the official measure set up for that purpose. . . . Some of the opponents of stabilization have sought to argue that while little Sweden could do so, big America could not. But so far as size is concerned the argument is obviously the other way. Sweden is so small as to be largely at the mercy of other countries. The United States is a world in itself. . . . Swedish foreign trade and the dependence of her exporters on foreign prices are far more serious than in the case of America." [1] Professor Fisher has mistaken the shadow for the substance. He attaches far too much importance to the stability of the Riksbank's index of the price level of consumption goods. The experience of Sweden resembles that of England in this respect. The policy was interesting merely because the Central Bank and the Treasury announced officially that they would keep the internal purchasing power of the krona constant. This declaration immediately after the break from gold tended to establish confidence. But it did not prevent a fall in production, real income, and employment. Our review of the monetary measures showed that in 1932 and 1933 the policy was changing its character. The aim was to secure a revival of investment; and this presupposed a rise in wholesale prices. An international margin became available as a result of currency depreciation, moderate duties on certain imports, and the increase in

[1] Irving Fisher, *Stabilized Money* (1934), pp. 408–9.

the demand for exports. The favourable balance was accompanied by loan expenditure on public works and an expansion in housing. It happened that stability of the krona-sterling rate of exchange did not interfere with the recovery programme. If sterling had appreciated in terms of gold, it is doubtful whether the Swedish authorities would have allowed the krona to follow suit. It also happened that the rise in capital values and wholesale prices did not push up the cost of living. The stability of the price level of consumers' goods was not affected by the recovery measures. The course of the index number was not a primary consideration influencing the actions of the Central Bank.

The monetary theory lying behind the so-called " Swedish experiment " gives no support to the naïve gospel of price stabilization preached by Professor Fisher. Nor is he justified in thinking that a policy which suits a small country is necessarily applicable to the United States. The theory of the international margin must be considerably modified in the case of a large country.

What weight are we to ascribe to the different factors in the recovery of Sweden? Depreciation of the currency, public investment financed out of loans, the rapid revival in the demand for exports, and the Central Bank's easy money policy all played a part.

Let us distinguish between the two sections of Sweden's economic system, namely the export of capital goods and the trades producing for internal consumption. By the middle of 1932 physical production in the former had fallen by 33 per cent but in the home industries the slump was only 15 per cent compared with the average of 1925–1930. Though the Central Bank did everything in its power to bring down rates of interest in 1933, the volume of investment remained stubbornly low. The Kreuger crash had shaken the confidence of the business world and producers were reluctant to undertake any new long-term commitments. Two factors prevented the slump from being more serious: the stimulus given to home industries by currency depreciation and the maintenance of consumers' income due chiefly to budget policy. Though some of Sweden's closest competitors also reduced the value of their currencies, there can be no doubt that the advantage to the export trades was more than temporary. Costs did not fall in the gold countries to correspond with the new rates of exchange. According to Professor Ohlin, Swedish " manufacturing industries did not at first regard the high quotations of foreign currencies as likely to be lasting, and therefore they did not dare to expand their productive capacity with a view to conquering a larger share of the home market. Only slowly did they grow accustomed to the idea that this foreign exchange relation might last for years." [1] The benefit got from currency depreciation was largely at the expense of other countries.

Even before the Labour Government introduced its unorthodox finance, the budget had not really been balanced. Accumulated funds were raided to the extent of 165 million kronor in the two financial years 1931–2 and 1932–3 in order to achieve equilibrium. The loan-financed public works appeared in the budget for the year July, 1933–June, 1934; but the actual outlay did not become effective until the first half of 1934. The amount borrowed by the State to buy up surplus stocks of wheat and rye was 30 million kronor in 1933 and 35 millions in 1934. Public investment could not have given any fillip to recovery in 1933.

Sweden could not avoid the pains of depression. We have seen that her pre-1929 prosperity was to a large extent a by-product of the inflation in the United States and Germany. Professor Myrdal is not justified in arguing that there were no unhealthy boom symptoms in Sweden before 1929. "The price level," he wrote, "during the whole period was gradually falling and speculation was kept within limits. In 1929 there were no indications of a crisis within Sweden." [2] Just as during

[1] B. Ohlin, "Economic Recovery and Labour Market Problems in Sweden," *International Labour Review*, May, 1935, p. 672.

[2] G. Myrdal, "Sverige och krisen," *Nationaløkonomisk Tidsskrift*, 1932, p. 2.

the War the pace had been set by the outside world, and when foreign conditions suddenly altered, the Swedish system was disturbed. A certain amount of liquidation was, therefore, necessary. But the Swedes wisely determined not to expiate sins which they had not committed. When the bottom fell out of the export market, a cumulative contraction would have spread through the home market industries as well, if drastic wage cuts and rigid economy had been the order of the day.

The Central Bank was successful in 1932 and 1933 in accumulating a large stock of foreign exchange and gold. The international margin even in 1933 would have permitted an ambitious policy of public works; and if this had been done the recovery of investment would have come sooner and the brake could have been applied towards the end of 1934. The Riksbank's measures and the Government's conversion schemes reduced the long-term rate to 3 per cent, which is 1 per cent below the pre-War level. But private investment did not respond automatically; and the demand for capital derived from the maintenance of activity in consumers' goods industries was a poor substitute for the collapse of foreign markets.

An inquiry by a Swedish bank into the position of 200 companies showed that in 1932 and 1933 they were busy reducing their indebtedness, and brought their loan capital below the level of 1929–1930.[1] This process began in the home market industries where the reductions were greatest. During the last three-quarters of 1933 as many industrial bonds were amortized as were issued. The improvement in the timber, pulp, and paper industries led to repayment of loans. The same inquiry revealed that industrial profits in 1932 were about a half of the 1929 figure: from that low point they advanced by 27 per cent in 1933. Whereas 77 per cent of the profits had been distributed in dividends in 1929, the proportions in 1932 and 1933 were 90 and 78 per cent respectively. This also had some effect in maintaining the demand for consumers' goods in the trough of the depression.

The second phase of the recovery—1934 and 1935—was dominated by other factors. Currency depreciation now played a minor part. Though wages had not been much reduced, a brisk demand for exports had set in. Wages and profits in the capital goods section rose rapidly; and the demand for consumers' goods, already well maintained, increased further. Within a comfortable international margin, the Government's loan expenditure on roads and bridges, electrification, and building had a stimulating effect. The price of capital

[1] See Dr. Karin Kock, *Konjunkturuppsvingets förlopp och orsaker* (Official Publications, 1935, No. 16), p. 44.

rose, and the private entrepreneur at last became optimistic. The average value of industrial and shipping shares (expressed as percentages of par) stood at 61·6 and 60·0 respectively in 1932 and 1933, and jumped to 75·7 in 1934 and 85·7 in the first nine months of 1935. The value of exports in 1934 was 350 million kronor more than in 1932. The recovery meant a change in the direction of investment. The demand for capital for use in home market industries is now more important, as shown by the output of wrought iron and building materials. The following comparison of the experience of Sweden, Norway, and Finland is of interest.

PRODUCTION IN HOME MARKET AND EXPORT INDUSTRIES IN SWEDEN, FINLAND, AND NORWAY[1]

(1929 = 100)

	Sweden.		*Finland.*		*Norway.*	
Year.	*Home market.*	*Export.*	*Home market.*	*Export.*	*Home market.*	*Export.*
1930 . . .	97	97	88	95	102	98
1931 . . .	89	78	77	87	83	70
1932 . . .	87	66	77	94	91	95
1933 . . .	88	72	89	107	92	98
1934 . . .	108	84	98	125	98	104

The revival of production in the home market in Sweden is more significant than the expansion of exports. The reverse is true of Finland and Norway. In Finland the weakness of the trade unions and the consequent flexibility of wages made her a strong competitor in the timber market.

The example of Sweden indicates that a

[1] *World Economic Survey, 1934–5* (League of Nations Economic Service), p. 122.

slump can be shortened and a recovery accelerated when the Government and the Central Bank co-operate to diminish uncertainty and to furnish the conditions necessary for a revival of investment. It would have been better if the loan expenditure on public works had been incurred in 1933, supplemented by a moderate reduction in wages. The international margin could then have been used to bring unemployment down to a minimum. The prosperity of 1935 is not free from instability. If the French franc were devalued it might lead to competition in currency depreciation which would upset Sweden's international margin. The demand for some of her exports might decline. This study has emphasized the fact that Sweden is closely bound up with the outside world. There will be instability as long as chaos reigns in international economic relations. Under present conditions Sweden can carry her rigid income structure without difficulty. But in the long run the continuance of her prosperity depends on a general revival in international trade and a removal of the grave political uncertainties which overshadow the continent.

STATISTICAL APPENDIX

I

The Swedish Budget, 1928–9 to 1935–6[1] (Million Kronor)

Expenditure

	Ordinary Budget. Current expenditure.	Ordinary Budget. Capital expenditure.	Ordinary Budget. Total.	Loan Budget. Expenditure financed by borrowing.	Grand Total.
1928–29	658·53	33·41	691·94	49·35	741·29
1929–30	689·29	55·62	744·90	34·41	779·31
1930–31	719·48	44·07	763·55	49·82	813·37
1931–32	760·89	55·56	816·45	72·80	889·25
1932–33	814·49	23·72	838·21	103·87	942·08
1933–34	720·37	39·48	759·85	269·49	1029·34
1934–35[2]	769·97	54·26	824·23	282·12	1106·35
1935–36[3]	866·79	62·02	928·81	136·64	1065·45

Revenue

	Ordinary Budget. Current revenue from taxes, etc.	Ordinary Budget. Income from State enterprises.	Ordinary Budget. Portion of profit of Bank of Sweden.	Ordinary Budget. Total of current revenue.	Ordinary Budget. Realization of capital assets.	Ordinary Budget. Total of ordinary Budget revenue.	Loan Budget. Loans.	Grand Total.
1928–29	560·24	115·53	13·90	689·67	2·27	691·94	49·35	741·29
1929–30	587·44	135·79	17·00	740·23	4·67	744·90	34·41	779·31
1930–31	595·17	141·70	19·00	755·87	7·68	763·55	49·82	813·37
1931–32	616·24	114·82	16·00	747·06	69·39	816·45	72·80	889·25
1932–33	656·79	94·99	14·00	765·78	72·43	838·21	103·87	949·08
1933–34	638·00	93·16	27·00	758·16	1·69	759·85	269·49	1029·34
1934–35[2]	711·37	105·28	7·00	823·65	0·58	824·23	282·12	1106·35
1935–36[2]	775·59	141·47	3·00	920·06	8·75	928·81	136·64	1065·45

[1] *Bilaga till 1935 års statsverksproposition : Inkomsterna (1935)*, p. 42.
[2] Provisional closed accounts.
[3] Estimates.

II

Indices of Swedish Recovery, 1933–5

	Volume of production.	*Volume of Production Home.*	*Volume of Production Export.*	*Wholesale prices.*	*Cost of living Riksbank Index.*	*Price of Imports.*	*Price of exports.*	*Yield of Government Bonds per cent.*	
	(1925–1930 = 100)			(1913 = 100)	(1931 = 100)	(1913 = 100)			
1929	110	107	116	140	—	126	144		4·56
1932—									
I	97	103	86	109	100·6	92	112		4·32
II	86	95	68	109	101·1	92	109		
III	83	87	67	109	101·1	95	107		
IV	85	85	87	109	100·6	97	108		
1933—									
I	89	90	87	106	99·7	92	104		4·02
II	85	90	76	106	98·9	93	108		
III	89	93	83	108	99·1	95	115		
IV	98	102	90	110	98·5	94	117		
1934—									
I	105	108	98	112	98·8	96	118	3·69	3·47
II	111	120	95	113	99·5	95	119	3·63	
III	110	118	97	114	99·4	96	120	3·50	
IV	113	119	102	115	99·5	95	117	3·06	
1935—									
I	118	123	107	115	100·0	95	116	3·04	3·19
II	119	128	100	115	100·5	96	113	3·15	
III [1]	—	—	—	115	100·9	97	114	3·23	
IV	—	—	—	118	100·8	102	116	3·34	

Source: *Ekonomisk Översikt* issued by the Swedish Board of Trade.

[1] A new index of production is under preparation.

III

The Swedish Balance of Payments,[1] 1933 and 1934 (Million Kronor)

Credit Items	Year 1933.	Year 1934.	Debit Items	Year 1933.	Year 1934.
I. Goods and Gold					
Exports	1,093	1,319	Imports	1,108	1,319
Gold, etc.	5	78	Gold, etc.	48	—
	1,098	1,397		1,156	1,319
II. Interest and Dividends					
Foreign Government Loans and other long-term investments	102	86	Swedish Government Loans, etc.	21	17
			Other long-term investments	4	5
Short-term investments	13	16	Short-term investments	12	13
	115	102		37	35
III. Miscellaneous					
Shipping freights	227	240	Swedish shipping outlay abroad	112	119
Emigrants remittances	20	12	Commissions, etc.	10	14
Foreign tourists	38	38	Swedish tourists' expenditure abroad	35	41
Other items	32	37	Other items	11	14
	317	327		168	188
Total of I, II, and III	1,530	1,826		1,361	1,542
IV. Capital Movements					
Export of Swedish Securities[2]	49	33	Import of Swedish Securities[2]	72	39
Export of Foreign Securities[2]	123	110	Import of Foreign Securities[2]	62	167
			Swedish participation in foreign flotations	1	1
Amortization on Swedish claims on foreign countries	18	16	Net Decrease in foreign short-term debts	32	[3]120
Net Increase in foreign short-term debts	116	12	Net Increase in foreign short-term assets	400	170
Net Decrease in foreign short-term assets	67	32			
	373	203		567	497
Total Balance					
Income and Capital Account	1,903	2,029		1,928	2,039
Difference[4]	25	10			
	1,928	2,039		1,928	2,039

[1] Based on *Kommersiella Meddelanden*, 1935, No. 18, pp. 567–581.
[2] Based on official but incomplete statistics.
[3] This figure includes an estimate of 80 million kronor, representing a reduction of the loan previously raised abroad for the purpose of protecting against exchange risks.
[4] This is due to the margin of error in the figures.

INDEX